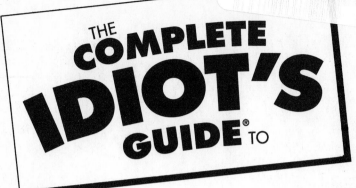

Christian Prayers and Devotions

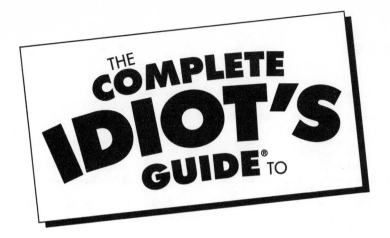

Christian Prayers
and Devotions

by James S. Bell Jr. and
Tracy Macon Sumner

ALPHA

A member of Penguin Group (USA) Inc.

ALPHA BOOKS

Published by the Penguin Group

Penguin Group (USA) Inc., 375 Hudson Street, New York, New York 10014, U.S.A.

Penguin Group (Canada), 10 Alcorn Avenue, Toronto, Ontario, Canada M4V 3B2 (a division of Pearson Penguin Canada Inc.)

Penguin Books Ltd., 80 Strand, London WC2R 0RL, England

Penguin Ireland, 25 St Stephen's Green, Dublin 2, Ireland (a division of Penguin Books Ltd.)

Penguin Group (Australia), 250 Camberwell Road, Camberwell, Victoria 3124, Australia (a division of Pearson Australia Group Pty. Ltd.)

Penguin Books India Pvt. Ltd., 11 Community Centre, Panchsheel Park, New Delhi—110 017, India

Penguin Group (NZ), cnr Airborne and Rosedale Roads, Albany, Auckland 1310, New Zealand (a division of Pearson New Zealand Ltd.)

Penguin Books (South Africa) (Pty.) Ltd., 24 Sturdee Avenue, Rosebank, Johannesburg 2196, South Africa

Penguin Books Ltd., Registered Offices: 80 Strand, London WC2R 0RL, England

Copyright © 2007 by James S. Bell Jr.

International Standard Book Number: 978-1-59257-582-4
Library of Congress Catalog Card Number: 2006932988

09 08 07   8 7 6 5 4 3 2 1

Interpretation of the printing code: The rightmost number of the first series of numbers is the year of the book's printing; the rightmost number of the second series of numbers is the number of the book's printing. For example, a printing code of 07-1 shows that the first printing occurred in 2007.

Printed in the United States of America

Most Alpha books are available at special quantity discounts for bulk purchases for sales promotions, premiums, fund-raising, or educational use. Special books, or book excerpts, can also be created to fit specific needs.

For details, write: Special Markets, Alpha Books, 375 Hudson Street, New York, NY 10014.

Publisher: *Marie Butler-Knight*

Editorial Director: *Mike Sanders*

Managing Editor: *Billy Fields*

Acquisitions Editor: *Michele Wells*

Development Editor: *Lynn Northrup*

Production Editor: *Kayla Dugger*

Copy Editor: *Keith Cline*

Cover Designer: *Bill Thomas*

Book Designers: *Trina Wurst/Kurt Owens*

Layout: *Chad Dressler*

Proofreader: *Terri Edwards*

Contents at a Glance

Contributor Table of Contents

Tracy Macon Sumner

Introduction

Two thousand years ago, a very special man we know as Jesus Christ walked the earth in a place called Palestine (now Israel), doing some incredible miracles and giving the best teaching ever when it came to the subject of faith in God.

In the fifth through seventh chapter of the Gospel of Matthew, we can read the best of the best of Jesus' teaching. Early in his earthly ministry, Jesus stood on a small hillside on the shores of the Sea of Galilee and delivered the world's most famous teaching, which has come to be known as his "Sermon on the Mount."

That day, Jesus told a big crowd of his followers, "pray like this":

"Our Father in heaven, may your name be honored. May your kingdom come soon. May your will be done here on earth, just as it is in heaven. Give us our food for today, and forgive us our sins, just as we have forgiven those who have sinned against us. And don't let us yield to temptation, but deliver us from the evil one." (Matthew 6:9–13)

Jesus wasn't telling his followers to just recite what has come to be known as "The Lord's Prayer" verbatim (although it's not necessarily a bad thing to do that). Instead he was offering this prayer as a model for his followers' personal communication with God. He wanted them to know that their prayers should always include words that honored God, submission to his will, requests that he meet their personal needs (physical and spiritual alike), confession of sin, and requests for personal strength when it came to sin.

In short, the Lord's Prayer was meant to be an outline for the prayers of a believer.

If you read through the four gospels—Matthew, Mark, Luke, and John—you will see that prayer played a key role in everything Jesus did and said. Jesus never went anywhere, did anything, or said anything without first knowing that it was the will of his Father in heaven. And how did he know that? Because he spent so much of his time in prayer.

It was prayer that gave him the wisdom from the Father for his teaching, the supernatural power for his miracles, and the strength to willingly die an agonizing death. In the same way, God wants us to pray to be able to know his will for our lives and have the strength to do it.

The Bible—Old and New Testaments alike—is filled with encouragements and commands for believers to pray. We need to understand that God wants us to pray for a couple key reasons. First, he wants us to have a personal relationship with him by talking to him daily ... about anything and everything that is on our minds and hearts. Second, God wants to bless us, guide us, forgive us, comfort us, and encourage us; and one of the ways he does that is through our communication with him through prayer.

But if you're like us, you find that prayer doesn't come easy. You get distracted, self-focused, at a loss for words, or fall into the same old routine. You know you're no match for the best of Christians. You don't need to be. You can use their prayers as starters and make them your own.

Most of the prayers in this book were written or spoken by people of the Christian faith throughout history. These saints, scholars, and ordinary people had the same struggles and desires that we have, and you'll be able to relate to both their reverence and honesty before God. Some of the prayers are themselves contained in liturgies or prayer books of the past, and we don't know the individuals who penned them. We particularly like Celtic prayers because of their simplicity and earthiness. The same is true for the prayers of Francis of Assisi.

We've taken the time to "adapt" these prayers into more reader-friendly, modern language (that means most of the thee's and thou's are gone, except in some poetry) so that you can more easily understand them and apply the ideas within the prayers to your personal life.

Some people like to pray and read early in the morning before they begin their day. Others like to have quiet time with God in the evenings or even just before they sleep. The set time should fit your temperament and schedule, but the point is to set up a regular schedule, or appointment with God, in order to have a consistent prayer and devotional life.

What You'll Find in This Book

This book contains some elements to help you better understand prayer and how it can become a wonderful blessing in your daily Christian life.

Each chapter contains prayers that pertain to a given topic—for example, thanksgiving, confession of sin, and prayers during times of trouble, just to name a few. If you're in a particular mood for thanksgiving or have a critical need—whatever the case—just open to the table of contents and begin at that page in the book. It's a quick-reference way to pray! This is not a book you need to read chronologically; you may approach it topically. You may want to pick prayers from critical things you need every day and then at certain times focus on the other topics.

Prayers in this book range from the ancient to the more modern, but it is heavily weighted toward the "classics." There are also some original prayers that we have penned. These prayers are identified with our names: James S. Bell, Jr. and Tracy Macon Sumner.

You'll also find "Short Memos to God" sidebars in each chapter. These short, one-thought prayers relate to the theme of the chapter and can be easily memorized or loosely remembered throughout the day. The Bible tells us to pray without ceasing, and some of the great men and women of old would pray them to stay close to God as they went about their daily affairs. The "Jesus Prayer" is an example of a famous prayer still used today: "Jesus Christ, Son of David, have mercy on me a sinner." We hope you'll find some of these short favorites handy, as a reminder of what you can say to God when you don't have this book. They do give you an idea of what to pray when it comes to a certain life situation or need. Asterisks between prayers denote another work by the same source. If a source is not listed, it means it's unknown.

We also include devotion boxes. These short writings—some adapted from classics Christian works and some original—allow you to better incorporate the given chapter topic into your ongoing relationship with God. These inspirational readings increase not only our understanding, but also our devotion to God. Devotional reading, like Bible reading and prayer, is a strong tradition in the spiritual lives of Christians throughout the ages. It is a companion to prayer that gives the reader something to meditate on and pray over. In the long run, we encourage you to pursue devotional books with similar readings to accompany your quiet times of prayer, along with Bible reading. This combination will provide the best helps to a one-on-one encounter with God.

Finally, at the back of the book, you'll find an appendix of sources, which provides information on the person (or other source) for the prayers in this book. This gives you a sense of context when it comes to reading these prayers in your personal prayer life.

Acknowledgments

I want to thank Michele Wells, acquisitions editor for this project, for allowing me to include a second book on prayer in this series. Thanks also to Lynn Northrup for her excellent editorial help. Finally, to my wife, Margaret, my daily prayer partner, who makes prayer, and God, come alive.

—JB

Special thanks go out to those who helped make this book happen. To my partner and co-author Jim Bell, I offer my thanks for his vision, for his direction, and for his own hard work on this project. To the good people at Alpha Books (and there are too many to list here), I say "thank you" for giving us this forum from which to encourage our readers to make prayer a big part of their daily lives.

Finally, I'd like to thank those (most of them posthumously) who originally offered up the prayers listed in this book. They reminded me that I go through nothing in my personal Christian life that someone hasn't gone through before me. I found that both encouraging and challenging —encouraging because I realized that truly am not alone in my walk with God, and challenging because I have seen the passion with which these men and women of God have prayed themselves through the very best and even the very worst in their own life situations.

—TS

Trademarks

All terms mentioned in this book that are known to be or are suspected of being trademarks or service marks have been appropriately capitalized. Alpha Books and Penguin Group (USA) Inc. cannot attest to the accuracy of this information. Use of a term in this book should not be regarded as affecting the validity of any trademark or service mark.

Part 1

Human-to-God "Relational" Prayers

At the heart of prayer is a personal relationship with the Creator of the universe, a God of love who wants His people to talk to Him daily. The first five chapters of this book cover different aspects of our relationship with God, including praise and worship, commitment and devotion, gratitude, God's grace and mercy, and our faith. All of these things are absolutely central to our relationship with God, and therefore central parts of any life of prayer.

Chapter 1

Prayers of Praise and Worship

The Westminster Larger Catechism, written in 1647 as a statement of the doctrine of the Christian faith, begins this way:

> *Question 1: What is the chief and highest end of man?*
>
> *Answer: Man's chief and highest end is to glorify God, and fully to enjoy him forever.*

The opening Q&A of the Westminster Larger Catechism reflects what the Bible tells us about our relationship with God. It is a personal, one-on-one relationship in which we have the privilege of praising and glorifying God through both word and deed and, in doing so, fully enjoying His presence.

In other words, God made and designed humankind so that we could be the one being in the entire world with whom He could enjoy a relationship based on love and fellowship. And how do we express our appreciation for that? Through praise and worship.

"We praise you, LORD," King David the psalmist wrote, "for all your glorious power. With music and singing we celebrate your mighty acts." (Psalm 21:13) This tells us that words of praise and worship aren't just acknowledgments of the goodness of God; they are indeed *celebrations* of the person of God Himself.

Christianity is filled with examples of men and women accepting God's invitation to fellowship with Him through words of praise and worship. Here are some of those prayers of praise and worship.

T. C. Chao

Oh Jesus, you do not need us to worship you as God. Without you we cannot know God, the creator and protector of the universe. We are unworthy, we should always learn from you. With you we have life, without you we are like lost sheep which have gone astray. We want you to be together with us, teacher, friend! We want to sing hymns of praise to you, offering you our sincere love and respect.

James S. Bell Jr.

Let everything that has breath praise the Lord, as the Psalmist records. Lord, you made us for yourself, help us to worship you with all of our minds, hearts, and strength. Let this not be a duty but a joy and delight. You are indeed worthy to receive honor, glory, praise, and thanksgiving for all you have done for us. Let us in our worship see the beauty of your holiness, for you indeed inhabit the praises of your people. We praise you along with the myriad number of angels and the saints whom you have redeemed in a heavenly chorus that shouts, "Hallelujah, for the Lord our God the Almighty reigns." We also say along with the church throughout the world, "Worthy is the Lamb, to receive honor and glory, riches and power, forever and ever. Amen."

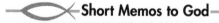

Short Memos to God

Fill my life, Lord my God,
In every part with praise,
That my whole being may proclaim
Your being and your ways.

—Horatius Bonar

John Baillie

I praise you for the life that stirs within me. I praise you for the bright and beautiful world into which I go. I praise you for earth and sea and sky, for scudding cloud and singing bird. I praise you for the work you have given me to do. I praise you for all that you have given me to fill my leisure hours. I praise you for my friends. I praise you for music and books and good company and all pure pleasures.

Carl Sandburg

Bless Thee, O Lord, for the living arc of the sky over me this morning.

Bless Thee, O Lord, for the companionship of night mist
far above the skyscraper peaks I saw when I woke once during the night.

Bless Thee, O Lord, for the miracle of light to my eyes
and the mystery of it ever changing.

Bless Thee, O Lord, for the laws Thou hast ordained holding fast
these tall oblongs of stone and steel, holding fast the planet Earth in its course and farther beyond the circle of the Sun.

Christina Rossetti

O Lord, the Lord whose ways are right, keep us in your mercy from lip-service and empty forms; from having a name that we live, but being dead. Help us to worship you by righteous deeds and lives of holiness; that our prayer also may be set forth in your sight as an incense, and the lifting up of our hands be an evening sacrifice.

Short Memos to God

Glory to you, God the Father, the Maker of the world. Glory be to you, God the Son, the Redeemer of mankind. Glory to you God the Holy Ghost, the sanctifier of your people.

—Brooke Foss Westcott

Louis Felici

Blessed be God. Blessed be his holy name. Blessed be the holy and undivided Trinity. Blessed be God the Father, maker of heaven and earth. Blessed be the holy name of Jesus. Blessed be Jesus Christ in his death and resurrection; on his throne of glory; in the atonement of his body and blood. Blessed be the Holy spirit, the giver and sustainer of life.

Isaac Watts

Give me the wings of faith to rise
within the veil, and see
the saints above, how great their joys,
how bright their glories be.

Once they were mourning here below,
and wet their couch with tears:
they wrestled hard, as we do now,
with sins, and doubts, and fears.

I ask them whence their victory came:
they, with united breath,
ascribe their conquest to the Lamb,
their triumph to his death.

They marked the footsteps that he trod,
his zeal inspired their breast;
and following their incarnate God,
possess the promised rest.

Our glorious Leader claims our praise
for his own pattern given;
while the long cloud of witnesses
show the same path to heaven.

Tracy Macon Sumner

I praise you, Lord, the God of love who has given your people a way to have perfect peace with you. I praise you, Lord, the God of forgiveness who wants to bury your people's sins in the depths of your intentional forgetfulness. I praise you, Lord, the God of perfect provision who has given your people everything they need to live the life you've give them to live. I praise you, Lord, the perfectly holy God who reaches down to such imperfect creatures as us.

George Herbert

King of glory, King of peace,
I will love Thee;
And that love may never cease,
I will move Thee.
Thou hast granted my request,
Thou hast heard me;
Thou didst note my working breast,
Thou hast spared me.

Wherefore with my utmost art
I will sing Thee,
And the cream of all my heart
I will bring Thee.
Though my sins against me cried,
Thou alone didst clear me;
And alone, when they replied,
Thou didst hear me.

Seven whole days, not one in seven,
I will praise Thee;
In my heart, though not in Heaven,
I can raise Thee.
Small it is, in this poor sort
To enroll Thee:
E'en eternity's too short
To extol Thee.

Lancelot Andrewes

Blessed are you, Lord, the God of our fathers, creator of the changes of day and night, giving rest to the weary, renewing the strength of those who are spent, presenting us occasions of song in the evening. As you have protected us this past day, so be with us in the coming night.

Always keep us from every sin, every evil, and every fear, for you are our light and salvation and the strength of our life. To you be glory for endless ages.

Short Memos to God

Blessing and honor, thanksgiving and praise, more than we can utter, more than we can conceive, be to you, most holy and glorious Trinity—Father, Son, and Holy Spirit—by all angels, all peoples, all creatures forever and ever.

—Lancelot Andrewes

Francis Xavier

My God, I love thee: not because
I hope for heaven thereby,
nor yet because who love thee not
are lost eternally.

Thou, O my Jesus, thou didst me
upon the cross embrace;
for me didst bear the nails and spear
and manifold disgrace.

And griefs and torments numberless
and sweat of agony;
even death itself—and all for one
who was thine enemy.

Then why, O blessed Jesus Christ,
should I not love thee well;
not for the sake of winning heaven
or of escaping hell;
not with the hope of gaining aught,
nor seeking a reward:
but as thyself has loved me,
O ever-loving Lord!

Even so I love thee, and will love
and in thy praise will sing,
solely because thou art my God
and my eternal king.

Teresa of Avila

You are great and wonderful, my Lord and my God. And yet we on earth are merely dull peasants if we imagined that we can understand something of you. That can surely be less than nothing, seeing that we are ignorant even of the great secrets within us. If I say "less than nothing," it is in comparison with the wonderful greatness that is in you, not because the splendors that we see aren't great, for it is through them that we can understand something of your works.

***

How great is your goodness, dear Lord! Blessed are you forever! May all created things praise you, God, for loving us so much that we can truthfully speak of your fellowship with humankind, even in this earthly exile. And however virtuous we may be, our virtue always depends on your great warmth and generosity, dear Lord. Your gifts are infinite.

How wonderful are your works!

Lifting Our Hearts in Praise

(Adapted from the writings of Lancelot Andrewes)

"In the year King Uzziah died, I saw the Lord. He was sitting on a lofty throne, and the train of his robe filled the Temple. Hovering around him were mighty seraphim, each with six wings. With two wings they covered their faces, with two they covered their feet, and with the remaining two they flew. In a great chorus they sang, 'Holy, holy, holy is the LORD Almighty! The whole earth is filled with his glory!'" (Isaiah 6:1–3)

This is an awesome scene of praise and worship for our God, spoken loudly and harmoniously by seraphim, angels whose only reason for being is to sing His praises. God made us, too, to enjoy

His presence by praising and worshiping Him. Where we differ from these beautiful creatures is that we *choose* to praise God from our hearts, with our mouths, and in our actions.

Lancelot Andrewes, the British post-Reformation Church of England bishop, wrote of reasons for praising God:

"Up with our hearts; we lift them to the Lord. O how very meet, and right, and fitting, and due, in all, and for all, at all times, places, manners, in every season, every spot, everywhere, always altogether, to remember him, to worship him, to confess to him, to praise him, to bless him, to hymn him, to give thanks to him, our maker, nourisher, guardian, governor, preserver, worker, per-fector of all, our Lord and Father, fountain of life and immortal-ity, treasure of everlasting goods, whom the heavens hymn, and the heaven of heavens, the angels and all the heavenly powers, one to another crying continually,–and we the while, weak, and unworthy, under their feet—Holy, Holy, Holy, Lord the God of Hosts; full is the whole heaven and the whole earth, of the maj-esty of his glory."

God doesn't make any of us praise Him. He has, however, given us the opportunity to be where He is simply because we make the choice to lift our voices and our hearts in praise to the God who truly deserves it.

Tracy Macon Sumner

Lord, thank you for designing us as the only created things who are able to praise you from our hearts and with our mouths. Thank you for allowing us to praise your name simply because we look at who you are and what you mean to us ... because we *want* to! Father, I don't always know how to praise you as you are worthy—what words to say, what actions to take—I ask that you make all my words and all my actions and make them into fitting praise to your name.

David M. Owen

Almighty God, our Father, help us to worship you sincerely, to listen to you attentively, and to respond to the teaching of your Spirit. Bless those appointed to special responsibilities of service, and ourselves as we share in it, for the glory of Jesus Christ our Lord.

Michelangelo

Lord, make me see your glory in every place: If mortal beauty sets my heart aglow, shall not that earthly fire by yours burn low extinguished by the great light of your grace? Dear Lord, I cry to you for help. Raise me from the misery of this blind woe. Your spirit alone can save me. Let it flow through will and sense, redeeming what is base. You have given me on earth this godlike soul, and a poor prisoner of it you have made behind weak flesh-walls; from that wretched state how can I rescue it, how my true life find? All goodness, Lord, must fail without your aid: For you alone have power to alter fate.

 **Short Memos to God**

God and Father of all, whom the whole heavens adore: let the whole earth also worship you, all kingdoms obey you, all tongues confess and bless you, and the sons of men love you and serve you in peace.
—Eric Milner-White

Julian of Norwich

Be a gardener. Dig a ditch, work and sweat, and turn the earth upside down and seek the deepness and water the plants in time. Continue this labor and make sweet floods to run and noble and abundant fruits to spring. Take this food and drink and carry it to God as your true worship.

Mechthild of Magdeburg

Burning mountain, chosen sun, perfect moon, fathomless well, unattainable height, unattainable light, clearness beyond all measure, wisdom without end, mercy without all limit, strength beyond resistance, crown of all majesty, all creation humbly sings your praise: Bright stars, high mountains, depths of the seas, rushing waters, all these break into song at heaven's proclamation: This is my Son, my beloved, my chosen one.

The Canticle of Brother Sun, Francis of Assisi

All praise be yours, my Lord, through all that you have made, and first my lord Brother Sun, who brings the day; and light you give to us through him. How beautiful he is, how radiant in all his splendor! Of you, Most High, he bears the likeness.

All praise be yours, my Lord, through Sister Moon and Stars; in the heavens you have made them, bright and precious and fair.

All praise be yours, my Lord, through Sister Water, so useful, lowly, precious, and pure.

All praise be yours, my Lord, through Brother Fire, through whom you brighten up the night. How beautiful he is, how gay! Full of power and strength.

All praise be yours, my Lord, through Sister Earth, our mother, who feeds us in her sovereignty and produces various fruits and colored flowers and herbs.

All praise be yours, my Lord, through Sister Death, from whose embrace no mortal can escape. Woe to those who die in mortal sin! Happy those she finds doing your will. The second death can do no harm to them.

Praise and bless my Lord, and give him thanks, and serve him with great humility.

***

You are holy, Lord, the only God, and your deeds are wonderful. You are strong. You are great. You are the Most High. You are Almighty.

You, holy Father are King of heaven and earth. You are Three and One, Lord God, all Good. You are Good, all Good, supreme Good, Lord God, living and true. You are love. You are wisdom. You are humility. You are endurance. You are rest. You are peace. You are joy and gladness. You are justice and moderation. You are all our riches, and you suffice for us. You are beauty. You are gentleness. You are our protector. You are our guardian and defender. You are our courage. You are our haven and our hope. You are our faith, our great consolation. You are our eternal life, Great and Wonderful Lord, God Almighty, Merciful Savior.

***

Holy, holy, holy, Lord God almighty, who is and who was and who is to come. Let us praise and exalt him forever and ever. Worthy are you, Lord our God, to receive praise, glory, honor, and blessing. Let us praise and exalt him above all forever. Worthy is the lamb that was slain to receive power and divinity, wisdom and strength, honor, glory, and blessing. Let us praise and exalt him above all forever. Let us bless the Father, the Son, and the Holy Spirit. Let us praise and exalt him above all forever. All the works of the Lord, now bless the Lord. Let us praise and exalt him above all forever. Praise God, all you his servants, and you that fear him, both small and great. Let us praise and exalt him above all forever. Let heaven and earth praise his glory, and every creature that is in heaven, and on earth, and under the earth. Let us praise and exalt him above all forever. Glory to the Father, and to the Son, and to the Holy Spirit, as it was in the beginning, is now, and shall be forever. Amen.

Short Memos to God

Lord, you are to be blessed and praised. All good things come from you. You are in our words and in our thoughts, and in all that we do. Amen.

—Teresa of Avila

Te Deum (Traditionally by Ambrose of Milan and Augustine of Hippo)

You are God: we praise you; you are the Lord; we acclaim you;
You are the eternal Father: all creation worships you.
To you all angels, all the powers of heaven,
Cherubim and Seraphim, sing in endless praise:
Holy, holy, holy Lord, God of power and might,
heaven and earth are full of your glory.
The glorious company of apostles praise you.
The noble fellowship of prophets praise you.
The white-robed army of martyrs praise you.
Throughout the world the holy Church acclaims you;
Father, of majesty unbounded,
your true and only Son, worthy of all worship,
and the Holy Spirit, advocate and guide.
You, Christ, are the king of glory,
the eternal Son of the Father.
When you became man to set us free
you did not shun the Virgin's womb.
You overcame the sting of death
and opened the kingdom of heaven to all believers.
You are seated at God's right hand in glory.
We believe that you will come and be our judge.
Come then, Lord, and help your people,
bought with the price of your own blood,
and bring us with your saints
to glory everlasting.

Edmund Rich

Lord, since you exist, we exist. Since you are beautiful, we are beautiful. Since you are good, we are good. By our existence we honor you. By our beauty we glorify you. By our goodness we love you. Lord, through your power all things were made. Through your wisdom all things are governed. Through your grace all things are sustained. Give us power to serve you, wisdom to discern your laws, and grace to obey those at all times.

Celtic Prayer of Praise, "Creation of the World"

My dear King, my own King, without pride, without sin, you created the whole world, eternal, victorious King.

King above the elements, King above the sun, King beneath the ocean, King of the north and south, the east and west, against you no enemy can prevail.

King of the Mysteries, you existed before the elements, before the sun was set in the sky, before the waters covered the ocean floor; beautiful King, you are without beginning and without end.

King, you created the daylight, and made the darkness; you are not arrogant or boastful, and yet strong and firm.

King, you created land out of shapeless mass, you carved the mountains and chiseled the valleys, and covered the earth with trees and grass.

King, you stretched out the sky above the earth, a perfect sphere like a perfect apple, and you decorated the sky with stars to shine at night.

King, you pierced the earth with springs from which pure water flows, to form streams and rivers across the land.

King, you ordained the eight winds, the four primary winds from north and south, east and west, and the four lesser winds that swirl hither and thither.

You gave each wind its own color: the north wind is white, bringing snow in winter; the south wind is red, carrying warmth in summer; the west wind is blue, a cooling breeze across the sea; the east wind is yellow, scorching in summer and bitter in winter; and the lesser winds are green, orange, purple, and black—the black wind that blows in the darkest nights.

King, you measured each object and each span within the universe: the heights of the mountains and the depths of the oceans; the distance from the sun to the moon, and from star to star.

You ordained the movements of every object: the sun to cross the sky each day, and the moon to rise each night; the clouds to carry rain from the sea, and the rivers to carry water back to the sea.

King, you divided the earth into three zones: the north cold and bitter; the south hot and dry; and the middle zone cool, wet, and fertile.

And you created men and women to be your stewards of the earth, always praising you for your boundless love.

Short Memos to God

I praise Thee while my days go on;
I love Thee while my days go on;
Through dark and dearth, through fire and frost,
With emptied arms and treasure lost,
I thank Thee while my days go on.

—Elizabeth Barrett Browning

Celtic Morning Prayer

The will of God be done by us;
The law of God be kept by us;
Our evil will controlled by us;
Our sharp tongue checked by us;
Quick forgiveness offered by us;
Speedy repentance made by us;
Angels' music heard by us;
God's highest praises sung by us.

Celtic Prayer of Praise

Hail to you, glorious Lord!
May church and chancel praise you,
May chancel and church praise you,
May plain and hillside praise you,
May the three springs praise you,
Two higher than the wind and one above the earth,
May darkness and light praise you,
May the cedar and the sweet fruit-tree praise you.

Abraham praised you, the founder of faith,
May life everlasting praise you,

May the birds and beasts praise you
May the stubble and the grass praise you.

Aaron and Moses praised you,
May male and female praise you,
May the seven days and the stars praise you,
May the lower and upper air praise you,
May books and letters praise you,
May the fish in the river praise you,
May the sand and the earth praise you,
May all good things created praise you,
And I too shall praise you, Lord of glory,
Hail to you, glorious Lord.

Nestorian Liturgy (Fourth or Fifth Century)

Worthy of praise from every mouth, confession from every tongue, and adoration and adulation from every living thing is the wonderful and glorious name of your glorious Trinity—Father, Son, and Holy Spirit—for you created the world in your grace and its inhabitants in your mercifulness. You saved men in your compassion, and showed great grace to mortals. Thousands upon thousands of those on high bow down and worship your majesty, my Lord, and ten thousand times ten thousand holy angels and spiritual hosts, the ministers of fire and spirit, glorify your name, and with holy cherubim and spiritual seraphim offer worship to your Lordship ....

Short Memos to God

Lord, praising you is a wonderful privilege. I thank you that you have chosen to make me an instrument of your praise. I thank you that you have chosen to share yourself with me that way.

—Tracy Macon Sumner

The Gloria (Based on Luke 2:14)

Glory to God in the highest, and on earth peace, goodwill toward men. We praise you. We bless you. We adore you. We glorify you. We give you thanks for your great glory. Lord God, heavenly King, God the Father almighty. Lord Jesus Christ, the only begotten Son. Lord God, Lamb of God, Son of the Father: you who take away the sins of the world, have mercy on us. You who take away the sins of the world, receive our prayer. You who sit at the right hand of the Father, have mercy on us. For you alone are holy. You alone are the Lord. You alone, Jesus Christ, are most high. Together with the Holy Spirit in the glory of God the Father.

Serapion of Thmuis

We praise you, Father, invisible, giver of immortality. You are the source of life and light, the source of all grace and truth; you love us all and you love the poor, you seek reconciliation with all and draw them all to you by sending your son to visit them, who now lives and reigns with you, Father, and the Holy Spirit, one God forever and ever. Amen.

 **Short Memos to God**

You are the guest who filled the jars with good wine. Fill my mouth with your praise.

—Ephraem of Syria

Augustine of Hippo

God, our true life, to know you is life, to serve you is perfect freedom, to enjoy you is a kingdom, to praise you is the joy and happiness of the soul. I praise and bless and adore you. I worship you, I glorify you. I give thanks to you for your great glory. I humbly beg you to live with me, to reign in me, to make this heart of mine a holy temple, a fit habitation for your divine majesty.

***

To you will I offer up an offering of praise. Late have I loved you, Beauty never old and ever new. You were within me and I without, and there I looked for You. You were with me when I was not with you. You called and cried to me, and pierced my deafness. You shined and glowed and dispelled my blindness. You touched me, and I burned for your peace.

Ephraem of Syria

What shall I give you, Lord, in return for all your kindness?
Glory to you for your love.
Glory to you for your mercy.
Glory to you for your patience.
Glory to you for forgiving us all our sins.
Glory to you for coming to save our souls.
Glory to you for your incarnation in the virgin's womb.
Glory to you for your bonds.
Glory to you for receiving the cut of the lash.
Glory to you for accepting mockery.
Glory to you for your crucifixion.
Glory to you for your burial.
Glory to you for your resurrection.
Glory to you who were preached to men and women.
Glory to you in whom they believed.
Glory to you who were taken up into heaven.
Glory to you who sit in great glory at the Father's right hand.
Glory to you whose will it is that the sinner should be saved through your great mercy and compassion.

Short Memos to God

O God who covers the high places with waters, who settles the sand as a boundary to the sea and upholds all things: the sun sings your praises, the moon gives you glory. Every creature offers a hymn to you, his author and creator forever.

—Eastern Orthodox Church

The "Rightness" of Praising God

(Adapted from the writings of John of Ruysbroeck)

"Praise the LORD! Give thanks to the LORD, for he is good! His faithful love endures forever." (Psalm 106:1)

It is right and good that we should thank and praise God because:

He has created us as reasonable creatures and has ordained and destined heaven and Earth and the angels to our service.

He became man for our sins, taught us, lived for our sake, and showed us the way.

He has ministered to us in humble clothing, suffered a shameful death out of love of us, and promised us His eternal kingdom and himself for our reward and our wage.

He has spared us in our sins, and has forgiven us or will forgive us, pouring His grace and His love into our souls.

He will live and remain with us, and in us, throughout all eternity.

He has visited us and will visit with us all the days of our lives with His noble sacrifices, according to the need of each, and has left us His flesh and His blood for food and drink, according to the desire and hunger of each.

He has set before us nature and the scriptures and all creatures, as examples, and as a mirror, so that we may look and learn how to make good works in everything we do.

He has given us health and strength and power and, when it is for our own good, sends us sickness.

When we have outward needs, He establishes inward peace and happiness within us.

He has caused us to be called Christian names and to have been born of Christian parents.

For all these things we should thank God here on Earth, so that afterward we may thank Him in eternity.

Chapter 2

Prayers of Commitment and Devotion to God

As Jesus prepared for his arrest and crucifixion, he called his disciples together and told them, "Remain in me, and I will remain in you. For a branch cannot produce fruit if it is severed from the vine, and you cannot be fruitful apart from me. Yes, I am the vine; you are the branches. Those who remain in me, and I in them, will produce much fruit. For apart from me you can do nothing." (John 15:4–5)

Jesus wanted the disciples to understand that their relationship with him, even after he returned to heaven, would be a loving relationship based on commitment—his commitment to them and their commitment to him. Without that commitment, there was no way his disciples—the original 12 as well as the ones to follow throughout the centuries—would to be able to live the way he'd instructed them to live and do the things he instructed them to do.

Commitment to God means doing the things it takes to have a growing, thriving relationship with Him. It means doing what He wants you to do and saying the things He wants you to say ... simply because you love him. It means believing that He is a God who keeps the promises He has made in His written Word, the Bible. It means making His desires your own desires.

In this chapter, we look at some prayers throughout the history of Christianity that demonstrate that kind of commitment.

Catherine Marshall

Come, Lord Jesus, and remain in my heart. How grateful I am to realize that the answer to my prayer does not depend on me at all. As I quietly remain in you and let your life flow into me, what freedom it is to know that the Father does not see my frayed patience or insufficient trust, rather only your patience, Lord, and your confidence that the Father has everything in hand. In your faith I thank you right now for a more glorious answer to my prayer than I can imagine.

Sadhu Sundar Singh

Lord God who is all in all to me, Life of my life and Spirit of my spirit, have mercy on me and fill me with your Holy Spirit and with love that there may be no room for anything else in my heart. I ask not for any blessing, but for you, who is the giver of all blessings and of all life. I ask not for the world and its pomp and glory, nor for heaven, but I need you yourself, for where you are, there is heaven. In you alone is satisfaction and abundance for my heart; you yourself, Creator, has created this heart for yourself, and not for any other created thing. Therefore this heart cannot find rest in anything but you: only in you, Father, who has made this longing for peace. So now take out of this heart whatever is opposed to you and abide and rule in it yourself.

Short Memos to God

Open my eyes that I may see, persuade my heart that I may desire, order my steps that I may follow the way of your commandments.

—Lancelot Andrewes

A. W. Tozer

Lord, teach me to listen. The times are noisy and my ears are weary with the thousand raucous sounds which continuously assault them. Give me the spirit of the boy Samuel when he said to you, "Speak, for your servant hears." Let me hear you speaking in my heart. Let me get used to the sound of your voice, that its tones may be familiar when the sounds of earth die away and the only sound will be the music of your speaking. Amen.

Charles de Foucauld

Father, I abandon myself into your hands; do with me what you will. Whatever you may do, I thank you. I am ready for all, I accept all. Let only your will be done in me, and in all your creatures—I wish no more than this, Lord. Into your hands I entrust my soul. I offer it to you with all the love of my heart, for I love you, Lord, and so need to give myself and to surrender myself into your hands, without reserve, and with unlimited confidence, for you are my Father.

Treasury of Devotion

Lord, I believe, but would believe more firmly. Lord, I love, but yet would love more warmly. I offer you my thoughts, that they may be toward you; my actions, that they may be according to you; my sufferings, that they may be for you.

Tracy Macon Sumner

Heavenly Father, I thank you that the only perfect place to be in this life is in a daily walk of commitment and devotion to you. May I always do and say the things that strengthen that commitment, and may you remove from me anything that keeps me from being completely and wholly devoted to you. May all that I do—be it work, recreation, relaxation—be fully devoted to you.

 **Short Memos to God**

Here, Lord, is my life. I place it on the altar today. Use it as you will.

—Albert Schweitzer

D. L. Moody

Our Heavenly Father, we pray that your blessing may rest on each one of us who profess to be Christians. Lord, help us to love Christ more than we love ourselves. Help us to be more like him in our way of life. Help us, Lord, to walk humbly, prayerfully, consistently on, in the dust of our pilgrimage so that men may not stumble over us and say, "They profess only, but they never do anything." God, help us to live up to what we profess, through you, in Christ Jesus, and may it be shown in each one of us.

***

Use me, my Savior, for whatever purpose and in whatever way you may require. Here is my sinful and troubled heart, an empty vessel. Fill it with your grace. Here is my sinful and troubled soul. Make it alive and refresh it with your love. Take my heart for your home, mouth to spread abroad the glory of your name, my love and all my powers for the advancement of your believing people. Never allow the steadiness and confidence of my faith to fade away—so that at all times I may be to say from the heart, "Jesus needs me, and I need him."

Short Memos to God

Our Father, teach us not only your will, but how to do it. Teach us the best way of doing the best thing, lest we spoil the end by unworthy means.

—John Henry Jowett

Frances Ridley Havergal

Take my life, and let it be consecrated, Lord, to thee.
Take my moments and my days; let them flow in ceaseless praise.
Take my hands, and let them move at the impulse of thy love.
Take my feet, and let them be swift and beautiful for thee.
Take my voice, and let me sing always, only, for my King.
Take my lips, and let them be filled with messages from thee.
Take my silver and my gold; not a mite would I withhold.
Take my intellect, and use every power as thou shalt choose.
Take my will, and make it thine; it shall be no longer mine.
Take my heart, it is thine own; it shall be thy royal throne.

Take my love, my Lord, I pour at thy feet its treasure store.
Take myself, and I will be ever, only, all for thee.

Short Memos to God

God of goodness, give me yourself. For you are sufficient
for me. If I were to ask for anything less I should always
be in want, for in you alone do I have all.

—Julian of Norwich

Jean-Baptiste Marie Vianney

I love you, my God, and my only desire is to love you until I draw my
last breath. I love you, my infinitely lovable God, and I would rather die
loving you than live without loving you. I love you, Lord, and the only
grace I ask is to love you eternally. ... My God, if my tongue cannot say
in every moment that I love you, I want my heart to repeat it to you as
often as I draw breath.

Committing Ourselves to the Love of God

(Adapted from the writings of François Fénelon)

"May you experience the love of Christ, though it is so great you
will never fully understand it. Then you will be filled with the
fullness of life and power that comes from God." (Ephesians 3:19)

It is sheer blindness to fear going too far when it comes to the
love of God. Let's take a close look at it. The more we love Him,
the more we love the things He has us doing. This is the love that
consoles us in our losses, that softens for us the crosses we must
bear, that separates us from that which is dangerous to love, that
preserves us from the thousands of things that are poisonous to
our souls, that shows us kind compassion when we are suffering,
that even in death opens for us eternal glory and happiness.

It is this love that changes all our evils to good, so why would
we fear filling ourselves too full of it? Are we afraid of being too
happy, or of being freed from ourselves, from the whims of our

pride, from the violence of our passions, and from the cruelty of this deceitful world?

Why do we wait to throw ourselves with full confidence into the arms of the Father of Mercies and the God of all consolation? He will love us, and we shall love Him. His love growing will take the place for us of everything else. He alone will fill our hearts, hearts the world has intoxicated, agitated, distressed—without being able to fill it. He will make us only feel contempt for a world for which we already feel contempt. He will take away from us the things that make us unhappy. He will make us do well what we were doing badly every day because we were not doing them for Him. He will make us do them well by inspiring us to do them out of obedience to Him. Everything—even the most mundane activities of a simple and ordinary life—will be turned to satisfaction, merit, and reward. We will even see the approach of death with peace, because we will see it as the beginning of eternal life.

Henry Martyn

Send your light and your truth so that we may always live near to you, our God. Let us feel your love, that we may be as though we were already in heaven, that we may do all our work as the angels do theirs. Let us be ready for every work, be ready to go out or come in, to stay or to depart, just as you shall appoint. Lord, let us have no will of our own, or consider our true happiness as depending in the slightest degree on anything that can happen to us outwardly, but as consisting altogether in conformity to your will.

Short Memos to God

Lord, take from me what keeps me from you. Lord, give me what brings me to you. Lord, take myself and give me yourself.

—Nicholas of Flüe

Elizabeth Ann Seton

Father, the first rule of our dear Savior's life was to do your will. Let his will of the present moment be the first rule of our daily life and work, with no other desire but for its most full and complete accomplishment. Help us to follow it faithfully, so that doing what you wish we will be pleasing to you.

***

Lord Jesus, who was born for us in a stable, lived for us a life of pain and sorrow, and died for us upon a cross; say for us in the hour of death, "Father, forgive," and to your mother, "Behold your child." Say to us, "This day you shall be with me in paradise." Dear Savior, never leave us or forsake us. We thirst for you, Fountain of Living Water. Our days pass quickly, and soon all will be accomplished for us. To your hands we commend our spirits, now and forever.

Eric Milner-White

Lord Christ, Lamb of God, Lord of Lords, call us, who are called to be saints, along the way of your cross. Draw us, who would draw, nearer our King to the foot of your cross. Cleanse us, who are not worthy to approach, with the pardon of your cross. Instruct us, the ignorant and blind, in the school of your cross. Bring us, in the fellowship of your sufferings, to the victory of your cross. And seal us in the kingdom of your glory among the servants of your cross, crucified Lord, who with the Father and the Holy Spirit lives and reigns, one God, almighty, eternal, world without end. Amen.

Short Memos to God

Lord, I shall be very busy this day. If I forget you, do not forget me.

—Sir Jacob Astley, prior to the Battle of Edgehill

Tracy Macon Sumner

Lord, there is no way that I can repay you for what you did for me when you sent your Son to die so that I could be forgiven. But remind me daily of the depth and breadth of your commitment and love to me so that I can demonstrate to you my own love and commitment, as imperfect as it is, in every part of my being.

John Wesley

Lord, take full possession of my heart. Raise there your throne and command from there as you do in heaven. Being created *by* you, let me live for you. Being created *for* you, let me always act for your glory. Being redeemed *by* you, let me give to you what is yours and let my spirit cling to you alone.

Blaise Pascal

Lord, from now on don't allow me to desire health or life except to spend them for you, with you and in you. You alone know what is good for me. Therefore, do what seems best to you. Give to me or take from me. Conform my will to yours, and grant that with humble and perfect submission and in holy confidence I may receive the orders of your eternal destiny and may equally love all that comes to me from you.

Short Memos to God

Jesus, fill me with your love now, and I ask you, accept me, and use me a little for your glory. Accept me and my service, and take for yourself all the glory.

—David Livingstone

John of the Cross

Flame of the Holy Spirit, you pierce the very substance of my soul and cauterize it with your heat. You love me so much that you have put into my heart the hope and the knowledge of eternal life. Earlier my prayers never reached your ears, because my love was so weak and impure. So although I desired you and begged you to warm my cold heart, you could not hear me. But now you have chosen to come to me, and my love burns with such passion that I know you hear my every prayer. I pray what you want me to pray. I desire what you want me to desire. I do what you want me to do. You have freed me to be your slave.

Teresa of Avila

For you I live and come to be—
What would you like done with me?

Sovereign, awful majesty,
Knowing till eternity—
Goodness, gracious to my soul,
Highness, godhead, one and whole,
Look at this nonentity
Singing of her love for thee—
What would you like done with me?

I am yours, because you made me,
Yours, because you then redeemed me,
Yours, because you suffered for me,
Yours, because you clamored for me,
Yours, because you did not lose me,
What would you like done with me?

What commands then, good my lord,
By such a creature should be done?
Or what office have I won,
Being but a slave abhorred?
Can't you see me, my sweet one?
Me, my sweet one, can't you see
What would you like done with me?

Right here is my heart, you see,
Lo, I put it in your hand,
My body, soul, all I command,
My entrails and my loving thee.
Redeemer sweet who married me,
Since I gave my all for thee,
What would you like done with me? ...

Be I silent, be I speaking,
Bearing fruit or bearing naught,
Let the Law show forth my fault,
Or Gospel soothe, if such you're seeking.
Be I gay, or by pain caught,
I only live when I'm with thee!
What would you like done with me?

For you I live and came to be—
What would you like done with me?

 **Short Memos to God**

Lord, take all of me—body, soul, and spirit—and use it as you see fit to glorify your name and help to draw others to you.
—Tracy Macon Sumner

James S. Bell Jr.

Father Almighty, creator of everything and the source of all that is good and satisfying, help us to be more devoted to you with all that we are and all that we have. Forgive my wandering, lustful heart that is always looking for something else to quench its insatiable thirst, when what I really desire is the grace to be more devoted to you and your Word. We have a "God-shaped hole" that can only be filled as we consecrate ourselves to your service. Let us be wholly set apart from all that desecrates, but rather consecrate both our inner and outer lives, our possessions, relationships, and careers, to the cause of Christ and His Kingdom. We pray that the spiritual disciplines of Bible study, meditation, fasting, good works, solitude, and corporate worship will be pleasing in your sight as we grow deeper in your love.

Book of Common Prayer, South Africa

Almighty God, who by your holy apostle has taught us to set our affections on things above, grant us so to labor in this life as ever to be mindful of our citizenship in those heavenly places where our Savior Christ has gone before; to whom with you, Father, and you, Holy Ghost, be all honor and glory, world without end.

Ignatius Loyola

Christ Jesus, when all is darkness and we feel our weakness and helplessness, give us the sense of your presence, your love, and your strength. Help us to have perfect trust in your protecting love and strengthening power, so that nothing may frighten or worry us, for, living close to you, we shall see your hand, your purpose, your will through all things.

Short Memos to God

God who has prepared for those who love you things so good that they surpass our understanding: pour into our hearts such love for you that we, loving you above all things, may obtain your promises, which surpass all that we can desire.

—The *Book of Common Prayer*

Peter Marshall

Our Father, sometimes you seem so far away, as if you are a God in hiding, as if you are determined to elude everyone who seeks you. Yet we know that you are far more willing to be found than we are to seek. You have promised, "If with all thy heart ye truly seek me, ye shall ever surely find me." And have you not assured us that you are with us always?

Erasmus of Rotterdam

Lord Jesus Christ, you have said that you are the Way, the Truth, and the Life: do not let us at any time stray from you, for you are our Way; or ever distrust your promises, for you are our Truth; or ever rest in anything other than you, for you are our Life. Lord Jesus, you have taught us what to believe, what to do, what to hope for, and in whom to take our rest.

***

Sever me from myself
that I may be grateful to you;
may I perish to myself
that I may be safe in you;
may I die to myself
that I may live in you;
may I wither to myself
that I may blossom in you;
may I be emptied of myself
that I may abound in you;
may I be nothing to myself
that I may be all to you.

Thomas à Kempis

Enlighten us, good Jesus, with the brightness of internal light and cast out all darkness from the home of our hearts. Grant us, Lord, to know what is worth knowing, to love what is worth loving, to praise what is worth praising, to hate what is unworthy in your sight, to prize what to you is precious, and, above all, to search out and do your holy will.

***

Who can tell what a day may bring forth? So cause me, God of grace, to live every day as if it were going to be my last, because for I all know it might be. Cause me to live now as I will wish I had lived when it is time for me to die. Grant that I may not die with any guilt on my conscience or any known sin I hadn't repented of, so that I may be found in Christ, who is my only Savior and Redeemer.

***

Write your blessed name, Lord, upon my heart, there to remain so indelibly engraved, that no prosperity, no adversity shall ever move me from your love. Be to me a strong tower of defense, a comforter in tribulation, a deliverer in distress, a very present help in trouble, and a guide to heaven through the many temptations and dangers in this life.

Short Memos to God

Most merciful redeemer, friend and brother, may I know you more clearly, love you more dearly, and follow you more nearly, day by day. Amen.

—Richard of Chichester

Catherine of Siena

You, eternal Father, Son, and Holy Spirit, are a deep sea, and the more I enter into it the more I find, and the more I find the more I seek. The soul cannot be satisfied without you, for she continually hungers for you, the eternal Trinity, desiring to see you with the light of your light. As the heart desires the springs of living water, so my soul desires to leave the prison of this dark body and see you in truth.

Eternal God, what more could you give me than yourself? You are the fire that burns without being consumed. You consume in your heat all the soul's self-love. You are the fire that takes away cold. With your light you illuminate me so that I may know all your truth. Clothe me with yourself, eternal truth, so that I may run this mortal life in true obedience, and with the light of your most holy faith.

Thomas Bradwardine

My God, I love you above all else, and I desire to end my life with you. Always and in all things with my whole heart and strength I seek you. If you do not give yourself to me, you give me nothing. If I do not find you, I find nothing. Grant, therefore, most gracious God, that I may always love you for your own sake more than anything else, that I may seek you always and everywhere in this present life, so that at the last I may find you and forever hold fast to you in the life to come.

Short Memos to God

Give what you will, and how much you will, and when you will. Set it where you will and deal with me in all things as you will.

—Thomas à Kempis

Edmund of Abingdon

Into your hands, Lord and Father, we commend our souls and our bodies, our parents and our homes, friends and servants, neighbors and
kindred, our benefactors and brethren departed, all your people faithfully believing, and all who need your pity and protection. Light us
with your holy grace and never let us be separated from you.

Anselm of Canterbury

Lord, because you have made me, I owe you all of my love. Because you
have redeemed me, I owe you all of myself. Because you have promised
so much, I owe you all of my being. Furthermore, I owe you as much
more love than myself as you are greater than I, for whom you gave
yourself and to whom you promised yourself. I pray, Lord, make me
taste by love what I taste by knowledge. Let me know by love what I
know by understanding. I owe you more than my whole self, but I have
no more, and by myself I cannot give the whole of it to you. Draw me
to you, Lord, in the fullness of love. I am wholly yours by creation.
Make me all yours, too, in love.

Short Memos to God

Lord, to you I dedicate myself. Accept me, and let me be
yours forever. Lord, I desire nothing else. I desire nothing
more.

—David Brainerd

The *Gelasian Sacramentary*

God who is the light of the minds that know you, the life of the souls
that love you, and the strength of the hearts that serve you: help us to
know you that we may truly love you, to truly love you that we may
fully serve you, whom to serve is perfect freedom.

Augustine of Hippo

Almighty God, in whom we live and move and have our being, you
have made us for yourself, and our hearts are restless until they find
their rest in you. Grant us purity of heart and strength of purpose so

that no other passion may hinder us from knowing your will, no weakness from doing it.

Meditations on Jesus Crucified

(Based on *Meditations on the Cross*, author unknown)

"For I decided to concentrate only on Jesus Christ and his death on the cross." (1 Corinthians 2:2)

Jesus, poor and abject, unknown and despised, have mercy upon me, and let me not be ashamed to follow thee.

O Jesus, hated, calumniated, and persecuted, have mercy upon me, and make me content to be as my master.

O Jesus, blasphemed, accused, and wrongfully condemned, have mercy upon me, and teach me to endure the contradiction of sinners.

O Jesus, clothed with a habit of reproach and shame, have mercy upon me, and let me not seek my own glory.

O Jesus, insulted, mocked, and spit upon, have mercy upon me, and let me not faint in the fiery trial.

O Jesus, crowned with thorns and hailed in derision; O Jesus, burdened with our sins and the curses of the people; O Jesus, affronted, outraged, buffeted, overwhelmed with injuries, griefs and humiliations; O Jesus, hanging on the accursed tree, bowing the head, giving up the ghost, have mercy upon me, and conform my whole soul to be thy holy, humble, suffering Spirit.

Chapter 3

Giving God Our Thanks

The Bible is filled with examples of people giving God thanks for various blessings. That includes this beloved psalm of thanksgiving:

"Shout with joy to the LORD, O earth! Worship the LORD with gladness. Come before him, singing with joy. Acknowledge that the LORD is God! He made us, and we are his. We are his people, the sheep of his pasture. Enter his gates with thanksgiving; go into his courts with praise. Give thanks to him and bless his name. For the LORD is good. His unfailing love continues forever, and his faithfulness continues to each generation." (Psalm 100)

God has identified Himself in the Bible as one who wants His people to thank Him—both verbally and in their actions—for the innumerable blessings He gives daily.

As believers, we have infinitely more to be thankful for than our minds can comprehend. That is reflected in these prayers of thanks.

William Barclay

I thank you for anything that happened to me that made me feel that life is really and truly worth living. I thank you for all the laughter that was in today. I thank you, too, for any moment when I saw the seriousness and the meaning of life. I thank you very specially for those I love, for those who love me, for all the difference it has made to me to know them, and for all the happiness it brings to me to be with them.

Louis Bromfield

Oh, Lord, I thank you for the privilege and gift of living in a world filled with beauty and excitement and variety. I thank you for the gift of loving and being loved, for the friendliness and understanding and beauty of the animals on the farm and in the forest and marshes, for the green of the trees, the sound of the waterfall, the darting beauty of the trout in the brook. I thank you for the delights of music and children, of other people's thoughts and conversation and their books to read by the fireside or in bed with the rain falling on the roof or the snow blowing past outside the window.

Short Memos to God

For each new morning with its light,
For rest and shelter of the night,
For health and food,
For love and friends,
For everything Thy goodness sends.
Father in heaven,
We thank thee.

—Ralph Waldo Emerson

John Henry Jowett

Thank you, Lord, for making all things beautiful in their time, and for putting eternity into our hearts. Most high Almighty, Good Lord God, creator of the universe, watch over us and keep us in the light of your presence. May our praise continually blend with that of all creation until we come to the eternal joys you lovingly promise. God our Father, we could thank you for all the bright things of life. Help us to see them, and to count them, and to remember them so that our lives may flow in ceaseless praise.

Walter Rauschenbusch

God, we thank you for this earth, our home, for the wide sky and the blessed sun, for the salt sea and the running water, for the everlasting hills and the whispering wind, for trees and common grass underfoot.

We thank you for our senses by which we hear the songs of birds, see the splendor of the summer fields, taste the autumn fruits, rejoice in the feel of snow, and smell the breath of the spring.

Grant us a heart opened wide to all this beauty, and save us from being so blind that we pass unseeing when even the common thorn bush is aflame with your glory.

Short Memos to God

Father, thank you for hearing me. You always hear me, but I said it out loud for the sake of all these people standing here, so they will believe you sent me.

—Jesus Christ (John 11:41–42)

Robert Louis Stevenson

Lord, behold our family here assembled.
We thank you for this place in which we dwell,
for the love that unites us,
for the peace accorded to us this day,
for the hope with which we expect the morrow;
for the health, the work, the food and the bright skies
that make our lives delightful;
for our friends in all parts of the earth. Amen.

 **Short Memos to God**

God, who has so greatly loved us, long sought us, and mercifully redeemed us, give us grace that in everything we may yield ourselves, our wills and our works, a continual offering of thanks to you.
—Westminster Confession of Faith

George Washington

Almighty God, and most merciful father, who commanded the children of Israel to offer a daily sacrifice to you, that through it they might glorify and praise you for your protection both night and day, receive, Lord, my morning sacrifice, which I now offer up to you. I give you humble and hearty thanks that you have preserved me from the danger of the past night and brought me to the light of the day—and its comforts—a day I devote to your service and your honor.

Vienna Cobb Anderson

God of all blessings, source of all life, giver of all grace, we thank you for the gift of life: for the breath that sustains life, for the food of this earth that nurtures life, for the love of family and friends without which there would be no life.

We thank you for the mystery of creation: for the beauty that the eye can see, for the joy that the ear may hear, for the unknown that we cannot behold filling the universe with wonder, for the expanse of space that draws us beyond the definitions of our selves.

We thank you for setting us in communities: for families who nurture our becoming, for friends who love us by choice, for companions at work, who share our burdens and daily tasks, for strangers who welcome us into their midst, for people from other lands who call us to grow in understanding, for children who lighten our moments with delight, for the unborn, who offer us hope for the future.

We thank you for this day: for life and one more day to love, for opportunity and one more day to work for justice and peace, for neighbors and one more person to love and by whom be loved, for your grace and one more experience of your presence, for your promise: to be with us, to be our God, and to give salvation.

For these, and all blessings, we give you thanks, eternal, loving God, through Jesus Christ we pray. Amen.

Tychon of Zadonsk

How shall I repay your generosity, my lover? How shall I repay my God for all he has given me? Had I died a thousand times for your sake, it would be nothing. That is because you are my Lord, my Creator and my God, and I am just clay and ashes, a sinner and a worthless servant who deserves all sorts of deaths, not just in this realm but in eternity. How shall I thank you, my Lord, my Lover, my Intercessor, my Liberator, my Redeemer? How shall I reward you, who did not spare yourself, but for my sake gave yourself up to dishonor, insult, mockery, infamy, to be spat upon, condemned, whipped, wounded, crucified, and put to death that I, a poor wretch, should be filled with joy? How shall I reward you? I have nothing I can call my own but my corruption, my helplessness, my sin. My soul and body—my nature—is from you and belongs to you. But, regrettably, I have corrupted and spoiled it myself. The temptations of the devil and my own desires have corrupted me.

I shall offer you a grateful heart, and that alone you desire of me. But even this thing I cannot do without you.

 **Short Memos to God**

And still, Lord, to me impart
An innocent and grateful heart.
—Samuel Taylor Coleridge

Joseph Addison

When all Thy mercies, O my God,
My rising soul surveys,
Transported with the view, I'm lost
In wonder, love and praise.

Thy Providence my life sustained,
And all my wants redressed,
While in the silent womb I lay,
And hung upon the breast.

To all my weak complaints and cries
Thy mercy lent an ear,
Ere yet my feeble thoughts had learned
To form themselves in prayer.

Unnumbered comforts to my soul
Thy tender care bestowed,
Before my infant heart conceived
From Whom those comforts flowed.

When in the slippery paths of youth
With heedless steps I ran,
Thine arm unseen conveyed me safe,
And led me up to man.

Through hidden dangers, toils, and deaths,
It gently cleared my way;
And through the pleasing snares of vice,
More to be feared than they.

O how shall words with equal warmth
The gratitude declare,
That glows within my ravished heart?
But thou canst read it there.

Thy bounteous hand with worldly bliss
Hath made my cup run o'er;
And, in a kind and faithful Friend,
Hath doubled all my store.

Ten thousand thousand precious gifts
My daily thanks employ;
Nor is the last a cheerful heart
That tastes those gifts with joy.

When worn with sickness, oft hast Thou
With health renewed my face;
And, when in sins and sorrows sunk,
Revived my soul with grace.

Through every period of my life
Thy goodness I'll pursue
And after death, in distant worlds,
The glorious theme renew.

When nature fails, and day and night
Divide Thy works no more,
My ever grateful heart, O Lord,
Thy mercy shall adore.

Through all eternity to Thee
A joyful song I'll raise;
For, oh, eternity's too short
To utter all Thy praise!

Giving Thanks ... for Things We Take for Granted

(By Tracy Macon Sumner)

"And you will always give thanks for everything to God the Father in the name of our Lord Jesus Christ." (Ephesians 5:20)

Thomas Traherne, the seventeenth-century British poet, once prayed:

"Is not sight a jewel? Is not hearing a treasure? Is not speech a glory? My Lord, pardon my ingratitude, and have sympathy on me because I am too slow to be sensible enough to appreciate these gifts. The freedom of your gift has deceived me. These things were too near for me to fully consider them. You presented me with your blessings and I was not aware of it. But now I give thanks and love and praise you for your immeasurable favors."

Traherne took to heart Paul's encouragement to "give thanks for everything to God the Father ..." and realized that he had neglected to thank God for some of the very basics in life, such as sight, hearing, and speech.

When most believers try to think of things to be thankful for, their minds immediately go to the sacrifice God made by sending

His Son, Jesus Christ, to come to earth to live then die a horrible death so that their sins can be forgiven.

Not a day should go by when we don't thank our heavenly Father for saving us by giving ... *everything*. We are who we are—children of the living God—and will be what we will be—living in his presence for all eternity—because of the work of Christ here on Earth, and a day should never go by when we don't offer Him thanks for that fact.

But as we take the time to humbly thank God for the biggest thing, our salvation, we should also look around us and within us to thank Him for those big and little things that are so easy to take for granted. That includes the senses He gave us—sight, smell, hearing, touch, and taste—that enable us to enjoy all that He has created for our benefit.

There is nothing God has given us for which we shouldn't make the conscious effort to thank and praise Him.

Anne Bradstreet

What shall I render to Thy name
Or how Thy praises speak?
My thanks how shall I testify?
O Lord, Thou know'st I'm weak.

I owe so much, so little can
Return unto Thy name,
Confusion seizes on my soul,
And I am filled with shame.

O Thou that hearest prayers, Lord,
To Thee shall come all flesh
Thou hast me heard and answered,
My plaints have had access.

What did I ask for but Thou gav'st?
What could I more desire?

But thankfulness even all my days
I humbly this require.

Thy mercies, Lord, have been so great
In number numberless,
Impossible for to recount
Or any way express.

O help Thy saints that sought Thy face
T' return unto Thee praise
And walk before Thee as they ought,
In strict and upright ways.

Tracy Macon Sumner

Lord, thank you for the gift of the beauty of nature. Thank you for
giving humankind places where they can get away and fellowship with
you as we meditate on the beauty of all you have made for us. As we get
away to enjoy being in those places, help us to never forget that they
are expressions of your love for each of us. Help us to remember that it
delights you to see us enjoying what you have made.

George Herbert

Thou that hast giv'n so much to me,
Give one thing more, a grateful heart.
See how thy beggar works on thee
By art.

He makes thy gifts occasion more,
And says, If he in this be crossed,
All thou hast giv'n him heretofore
Is lost.

But thou didst reckon, when at first
Thy word our hearts and hands did crave,
What it would come to at the worst
To save.

Perpetual knockings at thy door,
Tears sullying thy transparent rooms,

Gift upon gift, much would have more,
And comes.

This not withstanding, thou wentst on,
And didst allow us all our noise:
Nay thou hast made a sigh and groan
Thy joys.

Not that thou hast not still above
Much better tunes, than groans can make;
But that these country airs thy love
Did take.

Wherefore I cry, and cry again;
And in no quiet canst thou be,
Till I a thankful heart obtain
Of thee:

Not thankful, when it pleaseth me;
As if thy blessings had spare days:
But such a heart, whose pulse may be
Thy praise.

Lancelot Andrewes

To you, Jesus Christ, Word of the Father, we offer up our humble praises and sincerely cheerful thanks: who for love of our fallen race most wonderfully and humbly chose to be made man and to take our nature so that we might be born again by your Spirit and restored in the image of God. To you, blessed Trinity, be given all honor, might, majesty, and dominion, now and forever.

***

We thank you, our Lord, for our being, our life, our gift of reason. We thank you for nurturing us, preserving us, guiding us. We thank you for our education, our civil rights, our religious privileges. We thank you for your gifts of grace, of nature, of this world and for our redemption, our regeneration, our instruction in the Christian faith. We thank you for calling and recalling us and for your mercy and patience, which you have demonstrated so many times over so many years. We thank you for all the benefits we have received and all the prosperity you have given us in the things we do. We thank you for being able to use the blessings you have given us in this life.

For these and all other mercies, the ones we know about as well as the ones we don't, the ones that are out in the open and the ones you have given us in, the ones we remember and the ones we have forgotten, for the kindnesses we have received even when we didn't want it we praise you, we bless you, we thank you, every day.

Short Memos to God

We adore you, Lord Jesus Christ, in all the churches of the whole world and we bless you, for by means of your holy cross you have redeemed the world.

—Francis of Assisi

Teresa of Avila

How poorly we repay you, my Lord, for all the good things you have given us! In your majesty you seek all kinds of ways and means by which to show us the love that you have for us. Yet we hold this in low esteem because we are so inexperienced in loving you. Because we haven't practiced loving you as we should, our thoughts follow their usual pattern and we do not bother to ponder the great mysteries of the ways the Holy Spirit speaks to us. What more could he do to kindle our love for him and to urge us to contemplate that only with good reason was he moved to speak to us in the way he has?

***

Majestic King, forever wise,
You melt my heart, which once was cold,
And when your beauty fills my eyes
It makes them young, which once were old.

Christ, my creator, hear my cry,
I am yours, you can I hear,
My Savior, Lover, yours am I,
My heart to yours be ever near.

Whether in life or death's last hour,
If sickness, pain or health you give,
Or shame, or honor, weakness, power,
Thankful is the life I live.

John Knox

We give you honor and praise, Lord our God, for all the tender mercies
you so freely give to us throughout another week. Endless praise to you
for creating us in your image, for redeeming us by the precious blood
of your dear Son when we were lost, and for setting us apart through
your Holy Spirit. We thank you for your help and support in our times
of need, for your protection in the many dangers to body and soul, for
your comfort in our sorrows, for granting us the continued gift of life,
and for being so patient with us and giving us so much time to repent
of our sins. For these and all your blessings we have received only
because your goodness, we thank you and ask you to fill us continually with the Holy Spirit so that we can grow in your unmerited favor,
remain sure in our faith, and continue on in doing good.

Tracy Macon Sumner

Father, I thank you for reminding me daily that when you sent your
Son to die in my place so that I could be forgiven, you gave everything
you had for me. There is no greater love and sacrifice than that, and
there is no better gift than that of eternal life in your presence.

Phillip Melanchthon

We give you thanks, almighty, ever-living God of truth, eternal Father
of our Lord Jesus, creator of heaven and earth, of people and of all
creatures, sustainer of all things, source of all life, order and wisdom,
unfailing source of help: and to your Son our Lord Jesus Christ, your
Word and eternal image: and to your Holy Spirit, with whom you
endowed the apostles at Pentecost. We give thanks to you, God, fountain of grace and truth, wisdom and goodness, justice and mercy, purity
and loving kindness, for with wisdom unmatched you revealed yourself
to us, sending your Son into the world, who was destined to assume
human nature and to become a sacrifice for us.

We give thanks to you, Lord, for gathering your eternal church, for guarding the ministry of your Word, for granting your Holy Spirit and for giving everlasting life. We thank you, God, because you gave us all things, because you alleviated and removed the punishment we justly deserve, because you pour out upon us all the blessings of soul and body.

Short Memos to God

Dear Lord, I thank you for all the trials you have led me through, by which you prepared me to behold your glory. You have never forsaken nor forgotten me.

—Katherine von Bora

Mechthild of Magdeburg

Lord, I thank you that you have taken from me the sight of my eyes, and that now you serve me with the eyes of others. Lord, I thank you that you have taken from me the power of my hands, and that now you care for me by the hands of others. Lord, I prayed for them. Reward them in your heavenly love so that they may faithfully serve and please you until death.

James S. Bell Jr.

We thank you for this holiday that itself reminds us of the need for thanksgiving at all times. Our ancestors knew the source of their protection and blessing and set an example for us. Let us remember those who are less fortunate than us and give to them out of our abundance. May we take with us an "attitude of gratitude" that will be present throughout the entire year.

Bernard of Clairvaux

Jesus, how sweet is the very thought of you! You fill my heart with joy. The sweetness of your love surpasses the sweetness of honey. Nothing sweeter than you can be described. No words can express the joy of your love. Only those who have tasted your love for themselves can comprehend it. In your love you listen to all my prayers, even when my wishes are childish, my words confused, and my thoughts foolish. And you answer my prayers, not according to my own misguided desires, which would only bring me awful misery, but according to my real needs, which brings me sweet joy. Thank you, Jesus, for giving yourself to me.

Short Memos to God

O Lord, that lends me life, lend me a heart replete with thankfulness.

—William Shakespeare, from *Henry VI*

Anselm of Canterbury

Lord Jesus Christ, our Redeemer, our Salvation: we praise you and we give you thanks! And though we are unworthy of your gifts, and though we cannot offer to you a fitting devotion, yet let your loving kindness supply for our weakness.

Before you, Lord our God, all our desires are known, and whatsoever our heart rightly wills is a result of your grace. Grant that we may attain a genuine love of you. Don't let your grace be unfruitful in us, Lord! Perfect that which you have started! Give that which you have made us to long for. Convert our tepidity to fervent love of you, for the glory of your holy name.

Short Memos to God

Every time I think of you, I give thanks to my God. I always pray for you, and I make my requests with a heart full of joy because you have been my partners in spreading the Good News about Christ from the time you first heard it until now.

—The Apostle Paul (Philippians 1:3–5)

A Famous Anglican Prayer of Thanksgiving

Almighty God, Father of all mercies, we your unworthy servants give you most humble and hearty thanks for all your goodness and loving kindness to us and to everyone. We bless you for our creation, preservation, and all the blessings of this life. But above all, we thank you for your immeasurable love in the redemption of the world by our Lord Jesus Christ ...

And we humbly ask you, give us a due sense of all your mercies so that our hearts may be sincerely thankful and that we openly praise you, not only with our lips but in our lives by giving up ourselves to your service, by walking before you in holiness and righteousness all our days.

Tracy Macon Sumner

Father, remind me daily to express my thanks for all those "little" things you do for me. All of your gifts to me are good and perfect, so I want to remember to thank you for those things that are so easy to take for granted. Nothing you have done for me escapes my notice when I take the time to thank you for all you have done for me.

Anonymous Prayer of Thanks

Lord God, thank you for loving us even when we turn away from you. We are grateful for your constant care and concern. Thou we feel unworthy of your great love, we thank you that through our weakness you gave us strength, and in our wandering you show us the way.

Short Memos to God

You have given so much to us, give one more thing: a grateful heart, for Christ's sake.

—George Herbert

Irish Gaelic Prayer of Thanksgiving

Thanks to thee, O God, that I have risen today,
To the rising of this life itself;
May it be to thine own glory, O God of every gift,
And to the glory, aid thou my soul.

With the aiding of thine own mercy,
Even as I clothe my body with wool,
Cover thou my soul with the shadow of thy wing.

Help me to avoid every sin,
And the source of every sin to forsake,
And as the mist scatters on the crest of the hills,
May each ill haze clear from my soul, O God.

Augustine of Hippo

God, our true life, to know you is life, to serve you is freedom, to enjoy you is a kingdom, to praise you is the joy and happiness of the soul. I praise and bless and adore you. I worship you. I glorify you. I give thanks to you for your great glory. I humbly ask you to live with me, to reign in me, to make this heart of mine a holy temple, a fit habitation for your divine majesty.

Cultivating Gratefulness

(Adapted from *Morning and Evening*, by Charles Haddon Spurgeon)

"O Lord, you took up my case; you redeemed my life."
(Lamentations 3:58, New International Version)

Notice the positive tone of the prophet Jeremiah's words in this verse. He doesn't say, "I hope, I trust, I sometimes think ... that God took up my case," but speaks of it as an indisputable fact: "O Lord, you took up my case."

Likewise, we should, with the help of our gracious Comforter, lay aside the doubts and fears that so tarnish our peace and comfort. Our prayer should be that we are finished with the harsh croaking voice of presumption and suspicion and that we might be enabled to speak with the clear, musical voice of full assurance.

Notice how gratefully the prophet speaks as he gives all the glory to God alone. He doesn't speak a word about himself or his own pleadings. He doesn't credit his deliverance in any measure to any human, much less to his own merit. It is all about God!—
"O Lord, *you* took up my case; *you* redeemed my life."

The believer should always cultivate within himself or herself a grateful spirit. This is especially true after God has rescued or delivered us as only He can; then we should sing a song of thanks to our God. Earth should be a temple filled with the songs of grateful believers, and every day should be an altar smoking with the sweet incense of thanksgiving.

How joyful Jeremiah seems to be as he acknowledges the Lord's mercy! How triumphantly he lifts up his words of thanks! He has hit bottom (he has been called "the weeping prophet"), and yet ... we can hear his voice going up to heaven: "You took up my case; you redeemed my life."

As children of God, we should each seek after a real and vital experience of the Lord's love and kindness, and when we have it, we should speak positively of it, sing gratefully for it, and shout victoriously over it.

Chapter 4

God's Love, Grace, and Mercy

"But you, O Lord, are a merciful and gracious God, slow to get angry, full of unfailing love and truth," prayed King David in a prayer recorded in the eighty-sixth psalm.

At the foundation of the Christian faith is the belief in a loving God who poured out His grace and mercy on humankind by sending sent His Son, Jesus Christ, to earth to live and then die as a sacrifice for our sin.

The word *grace* has been given this thumbnail definition: God doing for us what we don't deserve. Likewise, mercy has been defined as God not doing to us what we do deserve. Both words have been summed up as "God's unmerited favor."

We can find throughout the Bible and throughout 2,000 years of Christian history many beautiful prayers acknowledging God's grace and mercy on those who know they are sinners in need of forgiveness and who also know that there is nothing they can do to earn those favors.

Pope John Paul II

Merciful Love, we pray to you, do not fail! Merciful Love, we pray
to you, be tireless! Be constantly greater than every evil, which is in
man and in the world. Be constantly greater than the evil which has
increased in our country and in our generation! Be more powerful with
the power of the crucified King! "Blessed be his kingdom which is
coming."

Short Memos to God

Grant, we beg you, merciful Lord, to your faithful people
pardon and peace, that they may be cleansed from all
their sins, and serve you with a quiet mind, through Jesus
Christ our Lord.

—The *Gelasian Sacramentary*

Dag Hammarskjöld

God whose I am, have mercy on us. Have mercy on our efforts so that,
in love and in faith and righteousness and humility, may follow you
with self-denial, steadfastness, and courage, and meet with you in the
silence.

Give us a pure heart that we may see you, a humble heart that we may
hear you, a heart of love that we may serve you, a heart of faith that we
may live you. You who I do not know but whose I am. You who I do not
comprehend but who hast dedicated me to my fate.

John Greenleaf Whittier

Pardon, Lord, the lips that dare
Shape in words a mortal's prayer! …

Not as one who seeks his home
With a step assured I come;
Still behind the tread I hear
Of my life-companion, Fear;
Still a shadow deep and vast
From my westering feet is cast,

Wavering, doubtful, undefined,
Never shapen nor outlined
From myself the fear has grown,
And the shadow is my own.

Yet, O Lord, through all a sense
Of Thy tender providence
Stays my failing heart on Thee,
And confirms the feeble knee;
And, at times, my worn feet press
Spaces of cool quietness,
Lilied whiteness shone upon
Not by light of moon or sun.

Hours there be of inmost calm,
Broken but by grateful psalm,
When I love Thee more than fear Thee,
And Thy blessed Christ seems near me,
With forgiving look, as when
He beheld the Magdalen.

Well I know that all things move
To the spheral rhythm of love—
That to Thee, O Lord of all!

Short Memos to God

Lord, it is my chief complaint,
That my love is weak and faint;
Yet I love you and adore,—
Oh! For grace to love you more!
—William Cowper

William Bright

Almighty God, from whom every good prayer comes, and who pours out on all who desire it the gift of grace and supplication, deliver us, when we draw close to you, from coldness of heart and wanderings of mind, that with steadfast thoughts and kindled affections we may worship you in spirit and in truth, through Jesus Christ our Lord.

Tracy Macon Sumner

Help us, Lord, to remember that it is only because of your amazing grace and incredible mercy that we are here today. We thank you for doing for us what we don't deserve and for not doing to us what we do. Help us to remember constantly the depths of your love and mercy and the wonder of your grace. Help us to demonstrate those things to those around us, those who are just as unworthy as we are.

Seraphim of Sarov

Lord, cleanse me of my sins and have mercy on me. You have created me—have mercy on me. There is no way to measure my sin—have mercy on me. Lord, forgive the many times I disobey you. Master, I bow down before your cross and glorify your resurrection. Lord, when I sin in what I say and do, have mercy on me because of your great compassion.

Short Memos to God

Lord God, though our sins be seven, though our sins be seventy-seven, though our sins be more in number the hairs on our head ... give us grace ... to cast ourselves down into the depths of your compassion.

—Christina Rossetti

John Bunyan

Lord, I have heard that you are a merciful God and have ordained that your Son Jesus Christ should be the Savior of the world; and, furthermore, that you are willing to give him to such a poor sinner as I am (and indeed I am a sinner): Lord, take therefore this opportunity and magnify your grace in the salvation of my soul, through your Son Jesus Christ.

James S. Bell Jr.

Words completely fail when we begin to express our deep appreciation to you for your amazing grace, your free and unmerited favor toward us who stand as less than perfect in your sight. You are a God who has many terms to describe your mercy—loving kindness, compassion, and long suffering. Thank you for your patience with our waywardness and weaknesses. You saved us when we were rebels and it is only your grace that lets us choose you over and over again. Please bestow your divine favor on the challenges we face and bless us spiritually, emotionally, and physically through our Lord Jesus Christ.

Thomas Ken

Blessing and honor, thanksgiving and praise more than we can utter be to you, most adorable Father, Son, and Holy Ghost, by all angels, all men, all creatures, forever and ever. To God the Father, who first loved us, and made us accepted and in Christ; to God the Son, who loved us, and used his own blood to wash away our sins; to God the Holy Spirit, who sheds the love of God abroad in our hearts be all love and all glory for time and eternity.

The Definition of Christ

(Adapted from the works of Martin Luther)

"… who gave himself for our sins to rescue us from the present evil age, according to the will of our God and Father." (Galatians 1:4, New International Version)

"[W]ho gave himself for our sins …." We know these things well—well enough as if we were actually touching the words— that we can easily talk of them. But in practice and in conflict— when the devil goes about trying to deface Christ and remove the work of grace out of our hearts—we find that we don't yet know them as well as we should.

He who can define Christ accurately during those times can look to him and see him as his most sweet savior and high priest, and not as a stern judge. That man has overcome all evils and is already in the kingdom of heaven. But to do this during times of conflict is the most difficult of all things to do. I speak from experience ….

This is why I so sincerely call upon you to learn the true and proper definition of Christ, as it appears in the words of Paul: "who gave himself for our sins." If Jesus gave himself to death for our sins, then he obviously is no tyrant or judge who will condemn us for our sins. He is not one to cast down the afflicted but one who raises up those who are fallen. He is a merciful reliever and comforter of those who are weighed down and broken hearted. Otherwise, Paul is lying when he says of Jesus, "who gave himself for our sins."

If I define Christ that way, I define him rightly and know and possess the true Christ indeed. I pass on all human speculations concerning his divine majesty, steady myself in the humanity of Christ, and therefore learn truly to know the will of God. There is no fear in knowing Christ this way, only total sweetness, joy, peace of consciences, and so forth. And in all these things there is a light opened, showing me the true knowledge of God, of myself, of all creatures, and of all the sin and depravity of the devil's kingdom.

This is not new teaching, but teaching that was established long ago, teaching the apostle and all godly teachers have taught us. God is willing that we could teach and establish these things that we might not only have them in our mouths but also well-grounded in the bottom of our hearts—and especially that we might be able to use them in the agony and conflict of death.

François Fénelon

You know better than I how much I love you, Lord. You know it and I don't, for nothing is more hidden from me than the depths of my own heart. I desire to love you and I fear not loving you enough. I beg you to grant me the fullness of pure love. See my desire: you have given it to me. See in me whom you created what you have placed there. God, you love me enough to inspire me to love you forever, so don't look at my sins. Look instead on your mercy and my love for you.

Tracy Macon Sumner

Jesus, you instructed your followers to pray that our Father would forgive our sins as we forgive those who sin against us. Sometimes, in my own human thinking, I don't know how you put up with some of the things your own people say and do. But you remind me daily that you don't base your mercy and forgiveness on our worthiness but on who you are; you forgive us for your own name's sake, because forgiveness and reconciliation are part of who you are.

King Charles I of England

Almighty and most merciful Father, look down upon us your unworthy servants, who here lay down before you at the footstool of your throne of grace. Look upon us, Father, through the arbitration and in the merits of Jesus Christ, in whom only you are well pleased, for in and of ourselves we are not good enough to stand before you. … We have broken your commandments in our thoughts, words, and deeds. We confess, Lord, that it is your mercy that endures forever and your compassion that never fails which is the reason we are still here. With you there is mercy and abundant redemption. In the abundance of your mercies and in the merits of Jesus Christ, don't give us the punishment we deserve, but instead be merciful to us and wash away all our sins with the precious blood which our Savior, which was shed for us. Purify our hearts by your Holy Spirit, and just as you add days to our lives, also, good Lord, we ask you to add repentance to our days so that when we reach the end of our lives we may fully enjoy your everlasting kingdom, all because of the merits of Jesus Christ our Lord.

Short Memos to God

Let us with gladsome mind
Praise the Lord, for his is kind;
For his mercies shall endure,
Ever faithful, for sure.

—John Milton

Teresa of Avila

My God, let me sing of your mercies for all eternity, since it has been your pleasure to so generously pour them out on me that those who see them are amazed. I myself wonder at them, and I can't help but burst into songs of praise to you, for alone and without you I should be nothing—like flowers uprooted from my garden while this miserable soil of mine is reduced again to the state of a dung-heap. Do not allow it, Lord! Do not let a soul that you have redeemed at such cost to be lost, a soul that so often you have turned to save and snatched from the throat of the devil, the fearful dragon.

Adapted from the Writings of Menno Simmons

O Lord of hosts! When I am kept afloat in the waters of your grace, I find that I cannot fully understand or appraise them, for your mercy is the greatest of all your works. Who, Lord, has ever come to you with a devout heart only to have you reject him? Who ever looked for you but didn't find you? Who ever wanted your help but didn't receive it? Who ever asked for grace and been denied? And who ever called on you that you didn't hear?

Sir Thomas More

Glorious God, give me grace to change my life and to see but not fear death, which for those know you is the gateway to an eternal life of wealth.

Good Lord, give me a humble, lowly, quiet, peaceable, patient, charitable, kind, tender, and pitiful mind, in all my works and all my words and all my thoughts, to have a taste of your holy, blessed Spirit.

Good Lord, give me a full faith, a firm hope, and a fervent charity, a love of you that can't be compared to my love for myself.

Good Lord, give me a longing to be with you, not to avoid the misfortunes of this world or just to arrive at that joyful place called heaven, but simply because I love you.

And give me, good Lord, your love and favor, which my love of you, however great it might be, doesn't and can't deserve if it weren't for your great goodness.

Good Lord, give me the grace to labor for these things that I pray for.

Short Memos to God

Grant, Lord, that we may live in your fear, die in your favor, rest in your peace, rise in your power and reign in your glory.

—William Laud

Thomas à Kempis

Most sweet and loving Lord, whom I now devoutly wish to receive, you know my weaknesses and my needs. You know how many bad habits and vices I have. You know how often I am burdened, tempted, shaken, and stained by sin. I come to you for healing. I pray to you for comfort and support. I speak to you, who know all things, to whom all my inmost thoughts are evident. You alone can adequately comfort me and help me. You know what good things I need most, and you know how poor I am in virtue.

Look at me, Lord! I stand before you poor and naked, asking for your grace and pleading for your mercy. Feed me, for I am hungry. Warm my coldness with the fire of your love. Illuminate my blindness with the light of your presence. Make all that leads me from you not worth thinking about. Make me forget it all. Lift up my heart to you in heaven, and let me not wander aimlessly about the world. From now on, you will be my only delight, for you alone are my food and drink, my love and joy, my sweetness and my whole good.

I desire that by your presence you would set me fully on fire, totally consume me and transform me into you, so that through the grace of inner union and by melting in love's flames I would become one spirit with you. Do not leave me hungry and thirsty, but treat me mercifully as you have so often and so admirably treated your saints. How wonderful it would be if I were burned and wholly consumed for you, since you are a fire always burning and never consuming, a love that purifies the heart and enlightens the mind.

Short Memos to God

Remember, Lord, what you have done in and for us is not what we deserve. And as you have called us to your service, make us worthy of that for which you have called us.

—*The Prayer Book*

Thomas Aquinas

Almighty and ever-living God, I approach the sacrifice of your only begotten Son, our Lord Jesus Christ. I come sick to the Doctor of Life, unclean to the Fountain of Mercy, blind to radiance of Eternal Light, and poor and needy to the Lord of heaven and earth.

Lord, in your great generosity heal my sickness, wash away my sin, enlighten my blindness, enrich my poverty, and clothe my nakedness. May I receive the Bread of Angels, the King of kings, and Lord of lords, with humble reverence, with the purity and faith, the repentance and love, and the determined purpose that will help to bring me to salvation. May I receive the sacrifice of the Lord's body and blood, and its reality and power. Kind God, may I receive the body of your only begotten Son, our Lord Jesus Christ, born from the womb of the Mary, and so be received into his spiritual body and numbered among his family members.

Short Memos to God

May God grant us his grace through our prayers to carry out our promises, through Jesus Christ our Lord.

—Leo the Great

Mechthild of Magdeburg

Dear Love of God, embrace this soul of mine, for it would sadden me bitterly to be apart from you. Therefore, I beg you not to let my love grow cold, for my works are worthless if I am not conscious of your presence.

Love, you make both pain and need sweet to me. You give wisdom and comfort to the children of God. Bond of Love, your hand is powerful, binding both young and old. You make the heaviest burdens light, even though our little sins to you are great. You serve all your creatures gladly for love alone.

Short Memos to God

Lord, we acknowledge your grace which created us. We praise your love which cares for us. And we worship your greatness which makes us glad, Lord of our death and our life.

—Nestorian prayer

Anselm of Canterbury

O merciful God, fill our hearts with the graces of your Holy Spirit—with love, joy, peace, long-suffering, gentleness, goodness, faith, humbleness, self-control.

Teach us to love those who hate us, to pray for those who despitefully use us so that we may be your children, our Father, who make your sun to shine on the evil and on the good and send rain on the just and on the unjust.

Tracy Macon Sumner

Where would I be, Lord, if it weren't for your grace and mercy? Where would I be if it weren't for the fact that you freely forgive those who confess their sins to you? Lord, I thank you for doing what in my human reasoning boggles my mind, namely forgiving me for even my worst offenses against you. Let me never forget to thank you for the wonderful gift of forgiveness.

Lord my God, grant us peace. Already, indeed, you have made us rich in all things. Give us the peace of being at rest, that Sabbath peace, the peace that knows no end.

—Augustine of Hippo

Alfred the Great

Lord God Almighty, shaper and ruler of all creatures, we pray for your great mercy, that you guide us better than we have done, toward you. And guide us to your will and to the need of our soul, better than we can ourselves. And steady our mind toward your will and to our soul's need. And strengthen us against the temptations of the devil. Put lust far away from us, as well as every unrighteousness. Shield us against our enemies, those we can see and those we can't. Teach us to do your will so that we may love you from the heart and with a pure mind before all things. For you are our maker and our redeemer, our help, our comfort, our trust, our hope. Praise and glory be to you now and forever.

Alcuin of York

Eternal Light, shine into our hearts,
Eternal Goodness, deliver us from evil,
Eternal Power, be our support,
Eternal Wisdom, scatter the darkness of our ignorance,
Eternal Pity, have mercy upon us; that with all our heart and mind and soul and strength we may seek your face
and be brought by thy infinite mercy to your holy presence;
through Jesus Christ our Lord.

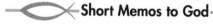

Glory to your infinite grace! The flood of your grace silences me and no movement is left in me, even to give due thanks.

—Isaac the Great of Syria

Gregory of Nyssa

Kindness flows from you, Lord, pure and continual. You had cast us off, as was only just, and mercifully you forgave us. You hated us, and you were reconciled to us. You cursed us, and then you blessed us. You banished us from paradise, and you called us back again. You took from us the fig leaves that had made had been for us such an unbecoming garment, and you put on us a cloak of great value. You opened the prison gates and gave the condemned a pardon. You sprinkled us with clean water and washed away the dirt.

Short Memos to God

O Lamb of God, who takes away the sin of the world, look upon us and have mercy upon us, you who is both victim and Priest, yourself both Reward and Redeemer.

—Irenaeus of Lyons

Understanding Sin ... and God's Grace

(Adapted from the works of John Bunyan)

"The proud Pharisee stood by himself and prayed this prayer: 'I thank you, God, that I am not a sinner like everyone else, especially like that tax collector over there! For I never cheat, I don't sin, I don't commit adultery, I fast twice a week, and I give you a tenth of my income.' But the tax collector stood at a distance and dared not even lift his eyes to heaven as he prayed. Instead, he beat his chest in sorrow, saying, '*O God, be merciful to me, for I am a sinner.*'" (Luke 18:11–13, italics added)

In his confession, the tax collector acknowledges that sin is the worst of all things, simply because it puts the soul in a place where no remedy can be found.

Nothing short of the mercy of God can deliver a poor soul from the terrible sickness of sin. But the Pharisee couldn't see this. No doubt he knew he had sinned at some time or other, but he had never come to a point in his life where he could see what sin was.

His knowledge of sin was that it was completely wrong, as we can see by his own cure for it: his own righteousness. It is undeniable truth that the Pharisee thought of himself as better than the tax gatherer before God because of his religious activities. For that reason, he never fully understood the truth about his own sin. That poor tax gatherer, however, understood his sin, as we can see from his response to God. He was driven to the only sovereign remedy for sin. Indeed, a proper understanding of sin—the guilt and filth, as well as its ability to condemn us—causes us to understand that nothing but God's grace and mercy through Jesus Christ can keep us from the hellish ruination sin brings.

Chapter 5

Prayers of Faith, Trust, and Reliance

"Lord, my heart is not proud; my eyes are not haughty. I don't concern myself with matters too great or awesome for me. But I have stilled and quieted myself, just as a small child is quiet with its mother. Yes, like a small child is my soul within me. O Israel, put your hope in the Lord—now and always." (Psalm 131)

In a very real way, King David's prayer of faith portended these words of Jesus Christ: "I assure you, unless you turn from your sins and become as little children, you will never get into the Kingdom of Heaven." (Matthew 18:3)

Jesus wanted his followers to understand that the faith that saved them was a childlike faith, the kind of faith in which the believer trusts God as a little child would trust her parents, meaning that the believer is to trust and rely on God just as a child relies on her mom and dad for everything she needs.

God desires more than anything that our relationship with Him be based in the kind of faith that moves us toward absolute trust and reliance in His ability and willingness to keep every one of His promises, to say to ourselves, "God said it, I believe it, and that settles it."

That is the kind of faith you will see demonstrated in the prayers in this chapter.

Book of Common Prayer, Canada

O Lord our heavenly Father, Almighty and everlasting God, who hast safely brought us to the beginning of this day: defend us in the same with your mighty power; and grant that this day we fall into no sin, neither fall into any kind of danger; but that all our doings may be ordered by thy governance, to do always that is righteous in your sight; through Jesus Christ our Lord. Amen.

Short Memos to God

Do, my God, stand by against all the world's wisdom and reason. Oh, do it! You must do it. Stand by me, true, eternal God!

—Martin Luther, on the eve of the Diet of Wörms

Thomas Merton

My Lord God, I have no idea where I am going. I do not see the road ahead of me. I cannot know for certain where it will end. Nor do I really know myself, and the fact that I think I am following your will does not mean that I am actually doing so.

But I believe that the desire to please you does in fact please you. And I hope that I have that desire in all that I am doing. And I know that if I do this, you will lead me by the right road though I may know nothing about it.

Therefore will I trust you always though I may seem to be lost and in the shadow of death, I will not fear, for you are ever with me, and you will never leave me to face my perils alone.

Short Memos to God

... hear me now, while kneeling here,
I lift to thee my heart and eye,
And all my soul ascends in prayer,
Oh, give me—give me faith! I cry.

—Anne Brontë

Celtic Prayer for God's Aid

God to enfold me,
God to surround me,
God in my speaking,
God in my thinking.

God in my sleeping,
God in my walking,
God in my watching,
God in my hoping.

God in my life,
God in my lips,
God in my hands,
God in my heart.

God in my sufficing,
God in my slumber,
God in mine ever-living soul,
God in mine eternity.

Henry Ward Beecher

We desire, Lord, that you will add to all our other gifts the gift of faith, by which we shall trust in you: faith that works by love; faith that stays with us; faith that transforms material things and gives them to us in spiritual meanings; faith that lights up the world with a light that never sets, that shines brighter than the day, that completely clears the night out of our experience. We humbly ask you to grant us faith that shall give us victory over the world and over ourselves and that makes us courageous in all temptation and makes us conquerors—*more* than conquerors through him who loved us.

Short Memos to God

Strong Son of God, immortal Love,
Whom we, that have not seen thy face,
By faith and faith alone embrace,
Believing where we cannot prove ....

—Alfred Lord Tennyson

Richard Challoner

My God, I believe in you, but strengthen my faith. All my hopes are in you, but do protect them. I love you, but teach me to love you daily more and more. I am sorry that I have offended you, but increase my sorrow.

I adore you as my first beginning and I aspire after you as my last end. I give you thanks as my constant benefactor, and I call upon you as my supreme protector.

Grant, my God, to conduct me by your wisdom, to control me by your justice, to comfort me by your mercy, to defend me by your power.

I desire to consecrate to you all my thoughts, words, actions, and sufferings that from now on I may think of you, speak of you, refer all my actions to your greater glory, and suffer willingly whatever you shall bring into my life.

Lord, I desire that in all things your will may be done because it is your will, and in the way that you will.

I beg you to enlighten my understanding, to inflame my will, to purify my body, and to sanctify my soul.

Tracy Macon Sumner

Lord, so many in this world live by that maxim, "God helps those who help themselves." But you are a God who helps those who know they are helpless without you, those who put their entire trust in you, those who know the truth of your words, "Without me, you can do nothing." Remind me, by whatever way you see fit, to rely on you for everything I have, everything I am, and everything you want me to be.

The Whole Duty of Man

Blessed Lord, whom without faith it is impossible to please, let your Spirit, I beg you, work in me such a faith as may be acceptable in your sight even such as works by love. Let me not rest in a dead, ineffectual faith, but grant that it may be the kind that shows itself in my good deeds, that it may be that victorious faith, which may enable me to overcome the world and conform me to the image of Christ, on whom I believe.

 **Short Memos to God**

Source and center of all being, grant us the gifts of your grace, that walking in your way and strengthened by your life, we may journey through this world in your peace, and rest in heaven with your saints.

—Gerhard Tersteegen

George Fox

Grant us, Lord, the blessing of those whose minds are focused on you so that we may be kept in perfect peace, a peace that cannot be broken. Don't let our minds rest on any created thing but only in the Creator. Don't let us focus our minds even on good things, houses, lands, inventions of vanities, or foolish fashions, lest our peace become broken and we become angry and weak and give over to envy.

James Pilkington

Hold us fast, Lord of Hosts, that we won't fall from you. Grant us thankful and obedient hearts, that our faith in the love, knowledge, and fear of you will increase daily. Increase our faith and help our unbelief, that we, being provided for and cared for in all our needs by your fatherly care and divine intervention … may live godly lives to the praise and good example of your people and after this life reign with you forever, through Christ our Savior.

The Knight's Prayer, from *A Book of Hours*

God be in my head,
And in my understanding;
God be in mine eyes,
And in my looking;
God be in my mouth,
And in my speaking;
God be in my heart,
And in my thinking;
God be at mine end,
And at my departing.

 **Short Memos to God**

Lord Jesus, help us to trust you even when we are going through the most trying times in our lives; to know that you are there with us and that your faithfulness is just.

—World Vision

Tracy Macon Sumner

Lord, on my own I can't forgive those who intentionally or carelessly hurt me, can't love those who I see as unlovable, can't keep my thoughts on you and off those things that just aren't important in the eternal realm of things. But I have learned that when I confess to you that "I can't," you have me where you want me: in a place of total dependence on you to do through me what I can't do myself.

Ignatius of Loyola

Take, Lord, all my liberty. Receive my memory, my understanding, and my whole will. All I have and possess you, Lord, have given to me. I now give it back to you, Lord. All of it is yours. Do with it as you will. Give me a love for you as well as your grace, for that is enough for me.

 **Short Memos to God**

Father in heaven, when the thought of you wakes in
our hearts, let it not wake like a frightened bird that flies
about in dismay but like a child waking from its sleep
with a heavenly smile.

—Søren Kierkegaard

Thomas Münzer

Just as a grain of wheat must die in the soil in order to yield a rich harvest, so your Son died on the cross to bring a rich harvest of love. Just
as the harvest of wheat must be ground into flour to make bread, so the
suffering of your Son brings us the bread of life. Just as bread gives our
bodies strength for our daily work, so the risen body of your Son gives
us strength to obey your laws.

James S. Bell Jr.

Our Father in heaven, when we think of faith we are reminded of the
verse in Hebrews that says without faith it's impossible to please you.
You have said that with the faith of a mustard seed we could move
mountains. Increase our faith—we believe but help our unbelief, as
the man who son was healed told Jesus. Give us spiritual eyes to see
evidence of your presence and your work in those around us and in the
everyday circumstances of life. Three things will remain forever—faith,
hope, and love—and faith is the foundation of all we have in you. Help
us to realize that doubts are healthy as we struggle to understand the
great mysteries of life and death, and turn our doubts and fears to faith
and confidence in your omnipotence on our behalf. All praise and glory
to you.

The Measuring Stick of Faith

(Adapted from the writings of Robert Haldane)

"As God's messenger, I give each of you this warning: Be honest in your estimate of yourselves, measuring your value by how
much faith God has given you." (Romans 12:3)

Speaking through the apostle Paul, God gives us here a standard by which we can evaluate ourselves. The word *faith* can mean a lot of things, but in this context, it means simply accepting and believing what God has told us in His written Word, the Bible.

By faith we are united to the Savior, and by faith we receive out of God's goodness all that He gives us. Therefore, the measure of faith with which each believer is blessed—whether it is strong or weak, great or small—shows with certainty both his or her true character before God and his or her relative standing among other believers. For that reason, every Christian should estimate himself or herself according to his or her faith, which is evidenced by the works he or she does.

The one who has the greatest faith is the highest in the school of Christ. The Bible teaches us that not only faith, but also every degree of it, is a gift from God. We believe because God has given us a measure of faith, and "to each one of us grace was given according to the measure of Christ's gift." (Ephesians 4:7)

When we read how Paul tells us to estimate ourselves, we will both be humble when it comes to self-esteem and also in our desire for the admiration of others. Because of that, we will be much less likely to become prideful and less likely to become discouraged.

Martin Luther

Behold, Lord, an empty vessel that needs to be filled. My Lord, fill it. I am weak in the faith; strengthen me. I am cold in love; warm me and make me passionate, that my love might go out to my neighbor. I do not have a strong and firm faith. At times I doubt, and am unable to trust you altogether. O Lord, help me.

Erasmus of Rotterdam

Lord Jesus Christ, you are the sun that always rises but never sets. You are the source of all life, creating and sustaining every living thing.

You are the source of all food, material and spiritual, nourishing us in both body and soul. You are the light that chases away the clouds of error and doubt, that goes before me every hour of the day, guiding my thoughts and my actions. May I walk in our light, be nourished by your food, be sustained by your mercy, and be warmed by your love.

Clare of Assisi

Glory and praise to you, most loving Jesus Christ, for the most sacred wound in your own side. By that adorable and holy wound you made known to the soldier Longinus, in the opening he made in your side, your infinite mercy. Most gentle Jesus, I ask you that, having redeemed me by baptism from the stain of original sin, now through your precious blood, which is offered and received throughout the world, deliver me from all evils, past, present, and future. By your most bitter death give me a lively faith, firm hope and a perfect charity, so that I may love you with my whole heart and with all my soul and strength. Make me carry on in your service, firm and unwavering in good works, so that I may be always able to please you.

Tracy Macon Sumner

Lord, when I read your Word, I can't help but see how unable I am to live out what it says. Remind me every day that in my own power, living and talking the way you call me to live in talk is an utter impossibility. Remind me that it is only through the power of your Holy Spirit that I can even come close to being all I can be in you. Show me every day areas in my life that I haven't given over to you, areas where I am not relying on you to do through me what I can't do for myself.

Anselm of Canterbury

Lord my God, teach my heart today where and how to see you, where and how to find you.

You have made me and remade me, and you have given me all the good things I have, but still I do not know you. I have not yet done that for which I was made.

Teach me to seek you, for I cannot seek you unless you teach me how, or find you unless you show yourself to me.

Let me seek you in my desire, and let me desire you in my seeking. Let me find you by loving you, and let me love you when I find you.

Short Memos to God

Almighty and eternal God, who controls all the world's affairs, there is no circumstance so great that it's not subject to your power, none so small that you don't care about it.

—Queen Anne of Great Britain and Ireland

Leofric, Bishop of Exeter

Lord, we ask you to keep your household, the church, in continual godliness so that through your protection it may be free from all adversity and earnestly given to serving you through good deeds that glorify your name.

Almighty God, to whom all hearts are opened, all desires known, and from whom no secrets are hidden, cleanse the thoughts of our hearts through the work of your Holy Spirit so that we may love you perfectly and rightly glorify your holy name.

Charles de Foucauld

Lord, grant us faith, the faith that removes the mask from the world and manifests God in all things, the faith that shows us Christ where our eyes see only a poor person, the faith that shows us the Savior where we feel only pain. Lord, grant us the faith that inspires us to undertake everything that God wants without hesitation, without shame, without fear, and without ever retreating; the faith that knows how to go through life with calm, peace, and profound joy, and that makes the soul completely indifferent to everything that is not you.

Short Memos to God

Each thing I received came from you. Each thing I hope for, from your love it will come. Each thing I enjoy is from you. Each thing I ask for comes because you want to give it to me.

—Alexander Carmichael

Alfred the Great of Wessex

Lord God Almighty, shaper and ruler of all creatures, we pray for your great mercy so that you may guide us, better than we have done, toward you. And guide us to your will, to our soul's need, better than we can ourselves. And steady our mind toward your will and to our soul's need. And strengthen us against the devil's temptations. Remove from us all wrong desires and all unrighteousness and shield us against our enemies, seen and unseen. And teach us to do your will so that we may inwardly love you above all things and with a pure mind. For you are our maker and our redeemer, our help, our comfort, our trust, our hope.

Isidore of Seville

Here we are in front of you, Holy Spirit. We feel the weight of our sicknesses, but we are united together in your name. Come to us, help us, enter into our hearts. Teach us what we should do, what path we should follow. Do for us what you ask us to do.

Be the only one to offer and guide our decisions, because only you—with the Father and the Son—have a glorious and holy name.

Do not allow us to miss out on doing what is right, you who loves order and peace. Don't let ignorance lead us away from you. Don't let human sympathy bias us. Don't let people or positions influence us.

Keep us intimately close to you, using the gift of your grace, so that we may be as one with you and so that nothing can separate us from your truth.

**Short Memos to God**

Lord, I praise you for this place I am in. But I have begun to wonder, is this the place you have for me? Hold me steady doing your will. It may be that I am just restless. If so, calm me and strengthen me so that I won't sin against you by doubting.

—Oswald Chambers

Prayer Attributed to Augustine of Hippo

Lord, for tomorrow and its needs,
I do not pray;
Keep me, my God, from stain of sin
Just for today.

Let me both diligently work,
And duly pray.
Let me be kind in word and deed,
Just for today.

Let me be slow to do my will,
Prompt to obey;
Help me to sacrifice myself
Just for today.

And if today my tide of life
Should ebb away,
Give me thy Sacraments divine,
Sweet Lord today.

So for tomorrow and its needs
I do not pray,
But keep me, guide me, love me, Lord,
Just for today.

A God We Can Trust in All Things

(Based on the writings of Thomas à Kempis)

"The LORD is my strength, my shield from every danger. I trust in him with all my heart. He helps me, and my heart is filled with joy. I burst out in songs of thanksgiving." (Psalm 28:7)

In what or whom can we place our trust in this life? What or who is the greatest comfort we can find on this earth? Isn't it our Lord and God, whose mercies we can't even count? Have we ever fared well with out Him? And how could anything go badly when He is there?

I would rather be poor with my God than rich without Him. I would rather wander the earth with Him than possess heaven without Him. Where He is, there is heaven; where He is not, there is death and hell. I want more of Him, so I must sigh and pray as I cry out to Him. There is no one but my God who I can fully trust to help me in all my needs. He is my hope, my confidence, my consoler. He is absolutely faithful to meet my every need.

People seek after their own interests. My God, however, places my salvation and my care first and makes all things work out for my benefit. Though He exposes me to various temptations and hardships, the God who proves His love daily to His loved ones in a thousand ways makes those things work for my good ....

That is why I place all my hope and my refuge in my Lord God. I cast all my troubles and anguish on Him, knowing that I have found everything but Him to be weak and untrustworthy. If my God does not help me Himself, having many friends or powerful helpers does me no good. Neither will wise counselors give useful answers, nor will the books of learned men console me, nor will gold or silver win my freedom, nor will any place—secret and beautiful as it may be—shelter me if God Himself doesn't help, comfort, console, instruct, and guard me. That is because everything that seems made for my peace and happiness is nothing—and truly offers no happiness—when He isn't there.

Indeed my God is the fountain of everything good. He is the best life has to offer, the most profound of all that can be said. Trusting in Him above everything else is the best comfort His servants can enjoy.

Part 2

Special Prayers in Life Situations

Within every Christian life are seasons when special prayers
are needed. The next four chapters cover some of those times,
including times of confession, suffering, the need for specific
provision, and for guidance. God desires to forgive us, comfort
us in our suffering, provide for us (physically, emotionally, and
spiritually), and guide us. All we need to do is ask! The prayers
that follow will give you an idea of how to pray through those
times in your life when you need a little something extra in your
prayer life.

Chapter 6

Prayers of Confession

In the Bible, God identifies Himself as a God of love, compassion, and forgiveness, a God who is more than willing to bury and forget the sins of those who come to Him in confession and repentance.

The Apostle John, who was one of Jesus' original 12 apostles, wrote, "But if we confess our sins to him, he is faithful and just to forgive us and to cleanse us from every wrong." (1 John 1:9) This verse is far from the only one in the Bible that tells us of God's willingness to forgive the penitent sinner. In fact, one of the best-known psalms is one of a sinner who seeks God's forgiveness and restoration.

This chapter looks at some famous prayers of confession from throughout Christian history.

David's Prayer of Repentance

David, a man the Bible calls "a man after God's own heart," had messed up—badly. He had committed adultery with Bathsheba, and then tried to cover up his sin by having her husband killed in battle. When the prophet Nathan confronted David about his sin, David was immediately filled with sorrow over what he had done. Here are his words of sorrow over his sin:

"Have mercy on me, O God, because of your unfailing love. Because of your great compassion, blot out the stain of my sins. Wash me clean from my guilt. Purify me from my sin. For I recognize my shameful deeds—they haunt me day and night.

"Against you, and you alone, have I sinned; I have done what is evil in your sight. You will be proved right in what you say, and your judgment against me is just. For I was born a sinner—yes, from the moment my mother conceived me.

"But you desire honesty from the heart, so you can teach me to be wise in my inmost being. Purify me from my sins, and I will be clean; wash me, and I will be whiter than snow.

"Oh, give me back my joy again; you have broken me—now let me rejoice. Don't keep looking at my sins. Remove the stain of my guilt. Create in me a clean heart, O God. Renew a right spirit within me. Do not banish me from your presence, and don't take your Holy Spirit from me.

"Restore to me again the joy of your salvation, and make me willing to obey you. Then I will teach your ways to sinners, and they will return to you. Forgive me for shedding blood, O God who saves; then I will joyfully sing of your forgiveness." (Psalm 51:1–14)

Coventry Cathedral Prayer

Father, forgive.
The hatred which divides nation from nation, race from race, class from class,

Father, forgive.
The covetous desires of people and nations to possess what is not their own,

Father, forgive.
The greed which exploits the labors of men and women and lays waste the earth,

Father, forgive.
Our envy of the welfare and happiness of others,

Father, forgive.
Our indifference to the plight of the homeless and the refugee,

Father, forgive.
The lust which dishonors the bodies of men, women and children,

Father, forgive.
The pride which leads us to trust in ourselves and not in God,

Father, forgive.

 **Short Memos to God**

Good shepherd, seek me out, and bring me home to your fold again. Deal favorably with me according to your good pleasure, so that I may dwell in your house all the days of my life and praise you forever and ever with those who are there.

—Saint Jerome

Book of Common Prayer, Church of Ireland

God, whose nature and property is ever to have mercy and to forgive, receive our humble petitions and, though we be tied and bound with the chain of our sins, yet let the compassion of your great mercy loose us; for the honor of Jesus Christ, our Mediator and Advocate.

Tracy Macon Sumner

Father, daily I sin in doing the things I know I should not and in not doing the things I know I should. Father, let me know beyond any doubt about the things about my character and actions that don't please you. As I bring those things to you in confession, I ask that you will forgive me and cleanse me and restore me to perfect fellowship with yourself. I further ask that you would make those things you call sin as distasteful to me as they already are to you.

Book of Common Prayer, Episcopal

Most merciful God, we confess that we have sinned against you in thought, word, and deed, by what we have done, and by what we have left undone. We have not loved you with our whole heart; we have not loved our neighbors as ourselves. We are truly sorry and we humbly repent, for the sake of your Son Jesus Christ, have mercy on us and forgive us; that we may delight in your will, and walk in your ways, to the glory of your name.

The *Book of Common Worship*

Almighty God, who does freely pardon all who repent and turn to Him, now fulfill in every contrite heart the promise of redeeming grace; forgiving all our sins, and cleansing us from an evil conscience; through the perfect sacrifice of Christ Jesus our Lord.

Short Memos to God

Grant us, Lord, such true repentance as may, through the blood of Jesus Christ our Savior, blot out the stains of our sins.

—Edmund Grindal

The Importance of Confession

(Adapted from *Morning and Evening,* by Charles Haddon Spurgeon)

"All of us have strayed away like sheep. We have left God's paths to follow our own. Yet the LORD laid on him the guilt and sins of us all." (Isaiah 53:6)

This is a confession of sin common to all people of God, those He calls His "elect." All of us have sinned, so we can say in one voice—from the first who entered heaven to the last who shall enter God's eternal kingdom—that "All of us have strayed away like sheep."

"We have left God's paths to follow our own" is a confession of the people of God as a whole and also as individuals. Each man and woman has within his or life a particular brand of sinfulness. Everyone sins, but each of us has sinful attitudes and actions other fellow believers don't struggle with.

Genuine repentance is marked with a natural association with others in that it naturally associates itself with those who express sorrow and remorse for their sins, but it also acknowledges the individuality of sin. "All of us have strayed away" is a confession that each of us have sinned individually against God in our own ways, in ways we can't see in others.

This kind of confession is complete and unqualified. There are no words spoken to soften its impact, and not so much as a syllable making excuses. This confession means giving up the idea that we are "good" in and of ourselves. It is the declaration of those who know they are guilty of sin and without excuse. It is confession where people stand before God, with their weapons of rebellion broken in pieces, and cry, "All of us have strayed away like sheep. We have left God's paths to follow our own."

This confession of sin is not accompanied by crying or sobbing, and that's because the next sentence makes it almost a song of celebration: "Yet the Lord laid on him the guilt and sins of us all." Of the three sentences in this verse, this is the most dreadful. But at the same time, it overflows with comfort. It is a paradox that where suffering was concentrated—on the cross—mercy also reigned, that where sorrow was at its worst, souls worn down by sin could find rest.

God bruised Jesus on the cross for our sins so that our bruised hearts could be healed. When we look intently at Jesus Christ on the cross and humbly confess our sins, we have confidence and healing through him.

James S. Bell Jr.

Father God, if we confess our sins, you are faithful and just to forgive all our sins and put us back in right relationship to you. We have sinned against you in thought, word, and deed. We have not loved you with our whole heart and have not loved our neighbor as ourselves. Create in us a clean heart and renew a right spirit within us, as the Psalmist David says. Wash us in the precious blood of the Lamb, and give us the grace to be set free from whatever sinful tendencies or bondages we may encounter. You who did not spare your only son for our sins will certainly forgive those who come to you with a sincere heart. Take away the guilt we experience and replace it with your peace and reconciliation.

Short Memos to God

Most merciful father, we come before your throne in the name of Jesus Christ, that for his sake alone you will have compassion on us, and not let our sins be a cloud between you and us.

—John Colet

John Greenleaf Whittier

Dear Lord and Father of mankind,
Forgive our foolish ways;
Reclothe us in our rightful mind,
In purer lives Thy service find,
In deeper reverence, praise.

Drop Thy still dews of quietness,
Till all our strivings cease;
Take from our souls the strain and stress,
And let our ordered lives confess
The beauty of Thy peace.

Breathe through the heats of our desire
Thy coolness and Thy balm;
Let sense be dumb, let flesh retire;
Speak through the earthquake, wind, and fire,
O still, small voice of calm.

Short Memos to God

Lord, discipline me for my sins and remove all evil from me. I am willing to endure any suffering here on earth, that I may be spared the torments of hell.

—Margery Kempe

Augustus Montague Toplady

Try me, God, and search the ground of my heart: prove me and examine my thoughts. Look and see if there is any wickedness in me, any root of bitterness yet undiscovered. Lead me in the way eternal. Show me the true state of my soul. Bring me out from every false refuge. Strip off every deceitful covering, every covering that is not of your Spirit. Forbid that the anchor of my hope should be cast, or the house of my dependence built, on any but Christ, the Rock of Ages. Forbid that I should rest short of that repentance which is your gift, and is connected with life eternal.

John Wesley

Forgive them all, Lord: our sins of omission and our sins of commission the sins of our youth and the sins of our riper years, the sins of our souls and the sins of our bodies, our secret and our more open sins, our sins of ignorance and surprise, and our more deliberate and presumptuous sins. Forgive the sins we have done to please ourselves and the sins we have done to please others, the sins we know and remember, and the sins we have forgotten. Forgive the sins we have tried to hide from others and the sins by which we have made others offend. Forgive them, Lord, forgive them all for the sake of the one who died for our sins, rose for our justification, and now stands at your right hand to make intercession for us, Jesus Christ, our Savior.

**Short Memos to God**

Almighty, forgive my doubt, my anger, my pride. By your mercy abase me, in your strictness raise me up.

—Dag Hammarskjöld

Charles Wesley

Times without number have I pray'd,
"This only once forgive";
Relapsing, when Thy hand was stay'd,
And suffer'd me to live.

Yet now the kingdom of Thy peace,
Lord, to my heart restore;
Forgive my vain repentances,
And bid me sin no more.

Short Memos to God

Son of God, do a miracle for me, and change my heart. Your having taken flesh to redeem me was more difficult than to transform my wickedness.

—Celtic prayer by Tadhg O'Huiginn

Anglican Prayer of General Confession

Almighty and most merciful Father, we have erred and strayed from your ways like lost sheep. We have followed too much the plans and desires of our own hearts and have broken your holy laws. We have left undone those things we should to have done, and we have done those things we should not have done. There is no health in us, but you, Lord, have mercy upon us miserable offenders. Spare them, God, who confess their faults. Restore them who are repentant, according to your promises declared unto mankind in Christ Jesus our Lord. And grant, most merciful Father, for his sake, that from now on we may live godly, righteous, and sober lives.

Short Memos to God

Our God, grant us grace to desire you with a whole heart, so that desiring you we may find you; and in loving you may hate those sins which separate us from you.

—Anselm of Canterbury

Teresa of Avila

How ashamed I am to see such sinfulness in myself, and to recall certain small things, mere grains of sand, which I nonetheless lacked the strength to lift off the ground out of love for you, embedded as they were in much wretchedness. And the water of your grace was not flowing beneath this and to raise it up.

My Creator, as I contemplate the great mercies I have received from you, I wish I could at least tell of some good act of mine, even though it would be of little significance in the midst of my great unfaithfulness.

Short Memos to God

Pardon, gracious Jesus, what we have been; with your holy discipline correct what we are. Order by your providence what we shall be; and in the end, crown your own gifts.

—John Wesley

Johann Arndt

Gracious and gentle and condescending God, God of peace, Father of mercy, God of all comfort; see, I grieve before you over the evil of my heart. I acknowledge that I am too prone to anger, jealousy, and revenge, to ambition and pride, which often give rise to conflict and bitter feelings between me and others. Too often in this way I have offended and grieved you, my longsuffering Father, as well as my neighbors. Forgive me this sin, and allow me to share in the blessing which you have promised to the peacemakers, who shall be called the children of God.

Tracy Macon Sumner

Father, thank you for your promise that if I confess my sins to you, you are faithful and righteous to forgive those sins. Reveal to me any sinful thing in myself, and help me not to rationalize or make excuses over them but instead to confess those things and to turn away from them. Help me to see not the momentary pleasure of my sin but instead the joy and peace of a life you yourself have cleansed.

Polycarp

Sweet Savior Christ, in your undeserved love for us you were prepared to suffer the painful death of the cross. Let me not be cold or even lukewarm in my love for you. Lord, help me to face the truth about myself. Help me to hear my words as others hear them, to see my face as others see me. Let me be honest enough to recognize my impatience and conceit. Let me recognize my anger and selfishness. Give me sufficient humility to accept my own weakness for what they are. Give me the grace—at least in your presence—to say, "I was wrong—forgive me." God, the Father of our Lord Jesus Christ, increase in us faith and truth and gentleness and grant us part and lot among the saints.

Ambrose of Milan

Lord Jesus Christ, I approach your banquet table in fear and trembling, for I am a sinner and dare not rely on my own worth but only on your goodness and mercy. I am corrupted by many sins in body and soul and by my careless thoughts and words. Gracious God of majesty and awe, I seek your protection and look for your healing. Poor troubled sinner that I am, I appeal to you, the fountain of all mercy. I cannot bear your judgment, but I trust in your salvation. Lord, I show my wounds to you and uncover my shame before you. I know my sins are many and great, and they fill me with fear, but I hope in your mercies, for they cannot be numbered.

Lord Jesus Christ, eternal King, God and Man, I pray, for I trust in you. Have mercy on me, full of sorrow and sin, for the depth of your compassion never ends. Praise to you, saving sacrifice, offered on the wood of the cross for me and for all mankind. Praise to the noble and precious blood, flowing from the wounds of my crucified Lord Jesus Christ and washing away the sins of the whole world.

Remember, Lord, your creature, whom you have redeemed with your blood. I repent of my sins, and I want to make right the wrong I have done. Merciful Father, take away all my offenses and sins. Purify me in body and soul.

Short Memos to God

Lord, who has mercy, take away from me my sins, and kindle in me the fire of your Holy Spirit. Give me a heart to love and adore you, to delight in you, to follow and enjoy you.

—Ambrose of Milan

Augustine of Hippo

Lord, the house of my soul is narrow; enlarge it that you may enter in. It is ruinous, O repair it! It displeases your sight; I confess it, I know. But who shall cleanse it, or to whom shall I cry but unto you? Cleanse me from my secret faults, Lord, and spare your servant from strange sins.

Saint Jerome

O Lord, show your mercy to me and gladden my heart. I am like the man on the way to Jericho who was overtaken by robbers, wounded and left for dead. Good Samaritan, come to my aid, I am like the sheep that went astray. Good Shepherd, seek me out and bring me home in accord with your will. Let me dwell in your house all the days of my life and praise you forever and ever with those who are there.

Melania the Younger

I have devoted my entire self to you, and taking me by your right hand you have led me with your counsel. But in my human frailty I have sinned both in word and deed many times against you, who alone are pure and without sin. Therefore, accept my prayer together with the tears I offer you through your holy ones, the victors in the arena, Purify me, this poor handmaid of yours, so that on departing toward you my passage may be hastened.

Prayer of Repentance, Orthodox Church

God, the lover of those who are unblemished and upright, grant us perfection in our hearts. Remove from us all evil and malicious thoughts. O Lord, open to us your merciful door, as you did to the thief. Accept our repentance as you had accepted the penance of the tax collector and the sinful woman. O Lord, you are merciful and pleased with those who turn to you in repentance as you graciously pardoned Peter who came to you after he had denied you. Lord cleanse us from our sins and follies.

O Lord! We, the sinful, grieve about your dispassionate last judgment. When the great books of accounts are opened and our sins are read, let your grace strengthen us and let your mercy help us. Let our sins be pardoned. O Lord! We acknowledge our sins, have mercy on us.

Alcuin of York

Almighty and merciful God, the fountain of all goodness, who knows the thoughts of our hearts, we confess that we have sinned against you, and done what you see as evil. Wash us, we implore you, from the stains of our past sins, and give us grace and power to put away all hurtful things so that, being delivered from the bondage of sin, we may produce the good fruits of repentance.

A Nigerian Believer's Prayer

God in heaven, you have helped my life to grow like a tree. Now something has happened. Satan, like a bird, has carried in one twig of his own choosing after another. Before I knew it he had built a dwelling place and was living in it. Tonight, my Father, I am throwing out both the bird and the nest.

Thomas Cranmer

Almighty and everlasting God, you hate nothing that you have made, and forgive the sins of all those who are penitent. Create and make in us new and contrite hearts that lamenting our sins and acknowledging our wretchedness, we may receive from you, the God of all mercy, perfect forgiveness and peace, through Jesus Christ our Lord. Amen.

Short Memos to God

Good Lord, give us true repentance to forgive us all our sins, negligences, and ignorances and to give us the grace of your Holy Spirit, to change our lives according to your holy Word.

—Thomas Cranmer

Richard Rolle

O Holy God, whose mercy and pity made thee descend from the high throne down into this world for our salvation: mercifully forgive us all the sins that we have done and thought and said. Send us cleanness of heart and purity of soul. Restore us with your Holy Spirit, that we may from now on live virtuously and love you with all our hearts, through Jesus Christ your son.

The Benefits of Confession

"Oh, what joy for those whose rebellion is forgiven, whose sin is put out of sight! Yes, what joy for those whose record the Lord has cleared of sin, whose lives are lived in complete honesty! When I refused to confess my sin, I was weak and miserable, and I groaned all day long. Day and night your hand of discipline was heavy on me. My strength evaporated like water in the summer heat. Finally, I confessed all my sins to you and stopped trying to hide them. I said to myself, "I will confess my rebellion to the Lord." And you forgave me! All my guilt is gone." (Psalm 32:1–5)

King David was a man who knew something about needing the forgiveness of God and freedom from guilt. And he was also a man who saw his own wrongdoing exactly as God sees it: as rebellion and sin.

David gives us a very unpleasant description of guilt before God because he refused to confess his sins. He tells us that he was "weak and miserable" and that he cried all day long and felt physically weak because God's hand of discipline was on him.

But when we read this entire passage, we see it as a psalm of thanksgiving, because David found inner peace, freedom from guilt, joy, and harmony with God—simply because he confessed his sins before a God who *wanted* to forgive him and cleanse him.

When we give ourselves to sin, we drive a wedge between ourselves and God. When that happens, it's often easy to shrink away from Him, believing that He's too disgusted and disappointed at us to want anything to do with us. But nothing could be further from the truth.

God has identified Himself to humankind as a loving creator who mourns when we fall into sin and who lovingly invites us to confess our sins to Him. When we do that, we receive the same benefits David received when he confessed: peace of mind, joy, and harmony with his creator.

Chapter 7

In Times of Crisis and Suffering

It has been wisely said that "there are no atheists in foxholes." Another way to say that is that when we are in a dangerous, difficult, or simply unpleasant situation, we are more prone than ever to pray to seek relief—and if not relief, then some answers.

King David once found himself in some extreme trouble. Absalom, his own son, was intent on overthrowing David's kingdom, and he had the support of a large segment of the population. This coup was successful at first, and David had to flee for his life while Absalom took the throne. It looked like the end of David's reign, except for one thing: God was on David's side. Here is David's prayer for protection in the face of this crisis:

"O Lord, I have so many enemies; so many are against me. So many are saying, 'God will never rescue him!' But you, O Lord, are a shield around me, my glory, and the one who lifts my head high. I cried out to the Lord, and he answered me from his holy mountain. I lay down and slept. I woke up in safety, for the Lord was watching over me. I am not afraid of ten thousand enemies who surround me on every side. Arise, O Lord! Rescue me, my God! Slap all my enemies in the face! Shatter the teeth of the wicked! Victory comes from you, O Lord. May your blessings rest on your people." (Psalm 3)

Throughout the Bible and Christian history alike, believers have prayed in the face of crisis. In this chapter, we look at some examples.

A Kenyan Revised Liturgy for Holy Communion

All our problems we send to the setting sun. All our difficulties we send to the setting sun. All the devil's works we send to the setting sun. All our hopes we set on the Risen Son. Christ the Sun of Righteousness shine upon you and scatter the darkness from before your path; and the blessing of God almighty, Father, Son, and Holy Spirit, be among you and remain with you always. Amen.

Short Memos to God

Grant that for your sake I may come to love and desire any hardship that puts me to the test, for salvation is brought to my soul when I undergo suffering and trouble for you.

—Thomas à Kempis

The Alphabet Prayer (Author Unknown)

Although things are not perfect
Because of trial or pain
Continue in thanksgiving
Do not begin to blame.
Even when the times are hard
Fierce winds are bound to blow
God is forever able
Hold on to what you know.
Imagine life without His love
Joy would cease to be
Keep thanking Him for all the things
Love imparts to thee.
Move out of "Camp Complaining"
No weapon that is known
On earth can yield the power
Praise can do alone
Quit looking at the future

Redeem the time at hand
Start every day with worship
To "thank" is a command.
Until we see Him coming
Victorious in the sky
We'll run the race with gratitude
Xalting God most high
Yes, there will be good times and yes some will be bad, but ...
Zion waits in glory ... where none are ever sad!
Amen!

Short Memos to God

Our God, who knows us to be set in the midst of so
many and great dangers, who knows that because of our
human frailty we can't always live upright lives: give us
the strength and protection to support us in all dangers,
and carry us through all temptations.
—The *Book of Common Prayer*

Rubem Alves

Lord: help us to see in the groaning of creation not death throes
but birth pangs; help us to see in suffering a promise for the future,
because it is a cry against the inhumanity of the present. Help us to
glimpse in protest the dawn of justice, in the cross the pathway to resurrection, and in suffering the seeds of joy.

Tracy Macon Sumner

Father, help me to see the difficulties in my life not as just chance
circumstances but as the instruments in your hand used to mold and
shape me into a stronger, more complete believer. Help me to see them
not just as your discipline, though sometimes they are, but as things
you have allowed into my life to help give me more strength, more
faith, more love, more compassion. In short, Father, use everything that
comes my way to draw me closer to yourself and to make me more and
more like your Son, my Savior Jesus Christ.

Dietrich Bonhoeffer

My God, early in the morning I cry to you. Help me to pray and to concentrate my thoughts on you: I cannot do this alone. In me there is darkness, but with you there is light; I am lonely, but you do not leave me; I am feeble in heart, but with you there is help; I am restless, but with you there is peace. In me there is bitterness, but with you patience; I do not understand your ways, but you know the way for me ....

Restore me to liberty, and enable me so to live now that I may answer before you and before humanity. Lord, whatever this day may bring, your name be praised.

***

Lord God, great distress has come upon me. My cares threaten to crush me, and I do not know what to do. Give me strength to bear what you send, and not let fear rule over me. Take a father's care of my wife and children.

Merciful God, forgive me all the sins that I have committed against you and against my fellow men. I trust in your grace and commit my life wholly into your hands. Do with me according to your will and as is best for me. Whether I live or die, I am with you, and you, my God are with me. Lord, I wait for your salvation and for your kingdom. Amen.

Short Memos to God

Father, if you are willing, please take this cup of suffering away from me. Yet I want your will, not mine.

—Jesus, as he prayed prior to his arrest (Luke 22:42)

Ravensbrück Concentration Camp, Found Beside a Dead Child

Lord, remember not only the men and women of goodwill, but also those of ill will. But do not remember all the suffering they have inflicted; remember the fruits we have bought; thanks to this suffering—our comradeship, our loyalty, our humility, our courage, our generosity, the greatness of heart which has grown out of all this, and when they come to judgment, let all the fruits which we have born be their forgiveness.

Book of Common Prayer, Scottish Episcopalian

Lord God, our heavenly Father, we pray that with your divine pity you see the pains your children endure. Grant that the passion of our Lord and his infinite love may make fruitful for good the tribulation of the innocent, the sufferings of the sick, and the sorrows of the bereaved.

James S. Bell Jr.

Lord, we thank you for your precious promise that when we call upon you in the day of trouble, you will deliver us and we will honor you. It seems trouble is never far enough away, it follows close on our heels, and it takes many forms. Sometimes it creates stress or fear, sometimes it involves suffering. We pray that will not allow the blessings from your Word to be choked by the cares of this world, as in the parable of the sower and the seed. Let us surrender to you in total dependence, gaining both your wisdom and power to handle difficult situations. We know that trials help to develop patience and purify us to become holy. Help us to remember that the trials of this life are nothing compared to the glory that will be revealed in the next life.

The Serenity Prayer (Attributed to Reinhold Niebuhr)

God, grant me the serenity to accept the things I cannot change, courage to change the things I can, and wisdom to know the difference. Living one day at a time; enjoying one moment at a time; accepting hardships as the pathway to peace; taking, as he did, this sinful world as it is, not as I would have it; trusting that he will make all things right if I surrender to his will; that I may be reasonably happy in this life and supremely happy with him forever in the next. Amen.

Abraham Lincoln, for a Nation at War

Grant, merciful God, that with malice toward none, with charity to all, with firmness in the right as you give us to see the right, we may strive to finish the work we are in: to bind up the nation's wounds, to care for those who have borne the battle, and for their widows and orphans, to do all which may achieve and cherish a just and lasting peace among ourselves and with all nations.

Short Memos to God

Give us the strength to encounter that which is to come, that we may be brave in peril, constant in tribulation, temperate in wrath, and in all changes of fortune, and down to the gates of death, loyal and loving one to another.

—Robert Louis Stevenson

Negro Spiritual

Nobody knows the trouble I see, nobody knows but Jesus. Nobody knows the trouble I see, Glory, Hallelujah! Sometimes I'm up, sometimes I'm down, O yes, Lord! Sometimes I'm almost to the groun', O yes, Lord. Nobody knows the trouble I see, nobody knows but Jesus. Nobody knows the trouble I see, Glory, Hallelujah!

Trials as Godly Correction

(Adapted from the writings of Philip Doddridge)

"For the Lord disciplines those he loves ...." (Hebrews 12:6)

Because "People are born for trouble as predictably as sparks fly upward from a fire" (Job 5:7) and because Adam's sin has caused the entire human race to inherit trouble on its way to death, we should all reasonably expect to meet with trials and tribulations in our own lives. Whoever you are, you should be prepared and in position to meet these trials, which you most certainly will encounter as a human being and as a Christian. You should be prepared to receive and endure these trials in a manner fitting not just as a man or woman, but also as a man or woman of God. ...

From the very moment your time of crisis comes—and there is no way you can escape life crises—you must never lose sight of the fact that God has a hand in it.... Your first response to crisis should be to "humble yourselves under the mighty power of God, and in his good time he will honor you." (1 Peter 5:6) If you believe that your trial is as a result of God's correction in your life, you should also personalize these words of an Old

Testament prophet: "Every time you punished us you were being just."(Nehemiah 9:33) Likewise, you should realize that when God disciplines you, He has "punished [you] far less than [you] deserve." (Ezra 9:13)

Finally, be ready and willing to endure God's hand of discipline patiently, glorify his name by submitting to His will.... Whatever form this discipline takes, be willing to endure it without grumbling and complaining.

Prayer of a Seriously Wounded Confederate Soldier

I asked God for strength, that I might achieve,
I was made weak, that I might learn humbly to obey.
I asked for health, that I might do great things,
I was given infirmity, that I might do better things.
I asked for riches, that I might be happy,
I was given poverty, that I might be wise.
I asked for power, that I might have the praise of men,
I was given weakness, that I might feel the need of God.
I asked for all things, that I might enjoy life, I was given life, that I might enjoy all things.
I got nothing that I asked for—but everything I had hoped for.
Almost despite myself my unspoken prayers were answered.
I am, among all men, most richly blessed.

J. R. Miller

God, our heavenly Father, we your children come now to your feet with our requests. We cannot live without your blessing. Life is too hard for us and the duty is too large. We come to you with our weakness, asking you for strength. Help us always to be cheerful. Give us grace to be encouragers of others, never discouragers. Let us not go about with sadness or fear among men, but may we be a blessing to every one we meet, always making life easier, never harder for those who come within our influence. Help us to be as Christ to others, that they may see something of his love in our lives and learn to love him in us.

Short Memos to God

O Lord, no one but you can help the powerless against the mighty! Help us, O Lord our God, for we trust in you alone. It is in your name that we have come against this vast horde. O Lord, you are our God; do not let mere men prevail against you!

—Asa (2 Chronicles 14:11)

Confidence, by Anne Brontë

Oppressed with sin and woe,
A burdened heart I bear,
Opposed by many a mighty foe;
But I will not despair.

With this polluted heart,
I dare to come to Thee,
Holy and mighty as Thou art,
For Thou wilt pardon me.

I feel that I am weak,
And prone to every sin;
But Thou who giv'st to those who seek,
Wilt give me strength within.

Far as this earth may be
From yonder starry skies;
Remoter still am I from Thee:
Yet Thou wilt not despise.

I need not fear my foes,
I need not yield to care;
I need not sink beneath my woes,
For Thou wilt answer prayer.

In my Redeemer's name,
I give myself to Thee;
And, all unworthy as I am,
My God will cherish me.

Short Memos to God

Lord, preserve us this day and strengthen us to bear whatever you see fit to lay on us, whether pain, sickness, danger, or distress; through Jesus Christ our Lord.

—Thomas Arnold

Madame Elizabeth of France, Written in Prison While Awaiting Death by Guillotine

I do not know, my God, what may happen to me today. I only know nothing will happen to me that you haven't foreseen from all eternity, and that is sufficient, my God, to keep me in peace. I adore your eternal designs. I submit to them with all my heart. I desire them all and accept them all. I make a sacrifice of everything. I unite this sacrifice to that of your dear Son, my Savior, begging you by his infinite merits, for the patience in troubles, and the perfect submission which is due to you in all that you will and design for me.

Tracy Macon Sumner

Lord, in the midst of difficulties, help us to look up from our own suffering, not just to ask "Why?" but also "What?" Remind us not just to ask you "why is this happening to me?"—though sometimes you will tell us when we ask—but "what do you want to do in and through this situation, Lord?" Teach us in everything to submit to your will, to your discipline, and to your teaching.

Robert Burns

O Thou Great Being! what Thou art,
Surpasses me to know;
Yet sure I am, that known to Thee
Are all Thy works below.

Thy creature here before Thee stands,
All wretched and distrest;
Yet sure those ills that wring my soul
Obey Thy high behest.

Sure, Thou, Almighty, canst not act
From cruelty or wrath!
O, free my weary eyes from tears,
Or close them fast in death!

But, if I must afflicted be,
To suit some wise design,
Then man my soul with firm resolves,
To bear and not repine!

Short Memos to God

Alone with none but thee, my God
I journey on my way.
What need I fear, when thou art near
O king of night and day?
More safe am I within thy hand
Than if an host didst round me stand.

—Saint Columba

John Woolman, in the Early Stages of Smallpox

Lord my God, the amazing horrors of darkness were gathered around me and covered me all over, and I saw no way to carry on. I felt the misery of my fellow creatures separated from the divine harmony, and it was heavier than I could bear, and I was crushed down under it. I lifted up my hand and stretched out my arm, but there was none to help me. I looked round about and was amazed. In the depth of misery, Lord, I remembered that you are all-powerful, that I had called you Father, and I felt that I loved you, and I was made quiet in your will, and I waited for deliverance from you. You had compassion on me when no man could help me. I saw that humility under suffering was showed to us in the most affecting example of your Son. You taught me to follow him, and I said, "Father, your will be done."

Short Memos to God

May Jesus Christ, the King of glory, help us to make the right use of all the suffering that comes to us and to offer to him the incense of a patient and trustful heart.
—Johannes Tauler

Claude de la Colombière

If I am to complain, let me complain to Jesus nailed to his cross. But in your presence, my Savior, what do have to complain about? What are my sufferings compared with those you bear without complaining? I might perhaps convince my fellow man that I am unjustly troubled, but in your presence, Lord, I cannot, for you know my sins. You know my sufferings are far less than I deserve. And since all my suffering proceeds from you, to you I come. Give me strength and hearten me to suffer in silence, as you did yourself.

Tracy Macon Sumner

Father, when I am going through difficulties of my own, bring to my path people who need to be comforted. When I am in emotional pain, bring those whose hearts are broken and in need of healing. Help me to understand that because you are with me, I never have to endure anything by myself. And help me to show others that when they have a brother or sister in Christ, they needn't be alone, either.

Ignatius of Loyola

Christ Jesus, when all is darkness and we feel our weakness and helplessness, give us the sense of your presence, your love, and your strength. Help us to have perfect trust in your protecting love and strengthening power, so that nothing may frighten or worry us, for, living close to you, we shall see your hand, your purpose, your will through all things. Amen.

Miles Coverdale

God, give us patience when the wicked hurt us. How impatient and angry we are when we think ourselves unjustly slandered, reviled and hurt! Christ suffers strokes upon his cheek, the innocent for the guilty, yet we may not stand up under one negative word for his sake. Lord, grant us virtue and patience, power and strength, that we may take all adversity with good will, and with a gentle mind overcome it. And if necessity and your honor require us to speak, grant that we may do so with gentleness and patience, that the truth and your glory may be defended.

Margery Kempe

Dear Lord, you suffered so much pain in order to save me and all mankind from sin. Yet I find it hard to bear even this little pain in my body. Lord, because of your great pain, have mercy on my little pain. And if you wish me simply to bear the pain, send me the patience and courage which I lack. It may seem strange to say it, but I would rather suffer the spiritual pain from the insults people hurl against me, in place of this physical pain. Indeed I enjoy spiritual pain suffered for your sake; and I happily embrace the disrespect of the world, so long as I am obeying your will. But in my feebleness, I cannot endure this present illness. Save me from it.

Short Memos to God

Help us to bear difficulty, pain, disappointment and sorrows, knowing that in your perfect working and design you can use such bitter experiences to shape our characters and make us more like our Lord.

—Ignatius of Antioch, before his martyrdom

Alcuin of York

Christ, why do you allow wars and massacres on earth? By what mysterious judgment do you allow innocent people to be cruelly slaughtered? I cannot know. I can only find assurance in the promise that your people will find peace in heaven, where no one makes war. As gold is purified by fire, so you purify souls by these bodily tribulations, making them ready to be received above the stars in your heavenly home.

Tracy Macon Sumner

Father, there are times in life when the suffering ask, "Where is God in all of this?" Help those of us who are strong in our faith to reach out to those who are going through difficulties, taking with us your message of love, compassion, and concern over anything and everything you call upon us to endure.

Augustine of Hippo

Dear Lord, watch with those who wake or watch or weep tonight and give your angels charge over those who sleep. Tend your sick ones, Lord Jesus Christ, rest your weary ones, bless your dying ones, soothe your suffering ones, shield your joyous ones, and all for your love's sake.

***

God of our life, there are days when the burdens we carry chafe our shoulders and weigh us down, when the road seems dreary and endless, when the skies are grey and threatening, when our lives have no music in them, when our hearts are lonely and our souls have lost their courage. Flood the path with light, run our eyes to where the skies are full of promise. Tune our hearts to brave music. Give us the sense of comradeship with heroes and saints of every age. Quicken our spirits so that we may be able to encourage the souls of all who journey with us on the road of life.

Polycarp, as He Awaited Execution at the Stake

Lord God Almighty, Father of your blessed and beloved child Jesus Christ, through whom we have received knowledge of you, God of angels and hosts and all creation, and of the whole race of the upright who live in your presence: I bless you that you have thought me worthy of this day and hour, to be numbered among the martyrs and share in the cup of Christ, for resurrection to eternal life, for soul and body in the incorruptibility of the Holy Spirit. Among them may I be accepted before you today, as a rich and acceptable sacrifice, just as you, the faithful and true God, have prepared and foreshown and brought about. For this reason and for all things I praise you, I bless you, I glorify you, through the eternal heavenly high priest Jesus Christ, your beloved child, through whom be glory to you, with him and the Holy Spirit, now and for the ages to come. Amen.

Short Memos to God

Comfort, merciful Father, by your word and Holy Spirit all who are afflicted or distressed, and so turn their hearts to you, that they may serve you in truth and bring forth fruit for your glory.

—Philip Melanchthon

The Prayer of Jehoshaphat

"O Lord, God of our ancestors, you alone are the God who is in heaven. You are ruler of all the kingdoms of the earth. You are powerful and mighty; no one can stand against you! O our God, did you not drive out those who lived in this land when your people arrived? And did you not give this land forever to the descendants of your friend Abraham? Your people settled here and built this Temple for you. They said, 'Whenever we are faced with any calamity such as war, disease, or famine, we can come to stand in your presence before this Temple where your name is honored. We can cry out to you to save us, and you will hear us and rescue us.' And now see what the armies of Ammon, Moab, and Mount Seir are doing. You would not let our ancestors invade those nations when Israel left Egypt, so they went around them and did not destroy them. Now see how they reward us! For they have come to throw us out of your land, which you gave us as an inheritance. O our God, won't you stop them? We are powerless against this mighty army that is about to attack us. We do not know what to do, but we are looking to you for help." (2 Chronicles 20:6–12)

Trust in Affliction

(Adapted from the writings of Philip Doddridge)

"Dear brothers and sisters, whenever trouble comes your way, let it be an opportunity for joy." (James 1:2)

God Himself has said, "No matter what happens, always be thankful." (1 Thessalonians 5:18) He also teaches us, His servants, to say, "We can rejoice, too, when we run into problems and trials." (Romans 5:3)

True believers can be assured that afflictions are tokens of God's mercy for "the Lord disciplines those He loves, and He punishes those He accepts as His children." (Hebrews 12:6) So you can see your troubles as loving discipline, and then realize that God's love deserves our praise.

When you are going through difficult times, say to yourself, "It is through these things that God is conforming me to the image of his Son. He is preparing me and training me for complete glory by removing any flaws in my character. He is making me a more gracious and patient person. He is working wisely to bring me nearer to Himself and to make me ready for His heavenly kingdom. Though His disciplines may not be pleasant, God certainly knows far better than I what I need. He knows exactly what I need in order to accomplish the very best in and for me, and He will graciously and lovingly accomplishing just that. This tribulation will help me "learn to endure. And endurance develops strength of character in us," as well as more confidence in Him. I will know beyond all doubt how much God loves me. (see Romans 5:3–5) God's love shines through my affliction like the sun through a cloud, sprinkling light upon the shade and mingling fruitfulness with my tears."

Chapter 8

Prayers for God's Provision

When we think of God's provision—which He has promised to all who put their trust in him—our minds most often go to our physical needs such as a roof over our heads, food to eat, and other life essentials.

But there are many other items that fall under the heading of what we think of as His "blessings." God also promises in His written word, the Bible, strength, protection, peace—the list goes on and on—for those who will just take the time to ask Him.

This chapter includes prayers asking for God's provision and blessing for a wide array of needs—physical and spiritual alike.

John Hunter

God our heavenly Father, in whom we live and move and have our being, have mercy upon all who are in poverty and distress. Be their help and defense, provide them with food and clothing sufficient for their bodily needs, and grant them day by day to cast all their care upon you. Help us in some way to help them.

Short Memos to God

You who give food to all flesh, which feeds the young ravens that cry to you, and has nourished us from our youth up: fill our hearts with good and gladness and establish our hearts with your grace.

—Lancelot Andrewes

John Henry Newman

May he support us all the day long, until the shades lengthen, and the evening comes, and the busy world is hushed, and the fever of life is over, and our work is done. Then in his mercy may he give us a safe lodging, and holy rest, and peace at last.

Charles Wesley

Shepherd Divine, our wants relieve
in this our evil day;
to all your tempted followers give
the power to watch and pray.

Long as our fiery trials last,
long as the cross we bear,
O let our souls on you be cast
in never-ceasing prayer.

The Spirit's interceding grace
give us in faith to claim;
to wrestle till we see thy face,
and know your hidden Name.

Till your perfect love impart,
till you yourself bestow,
be this the cry of every heart,
"I will not let you go."

I will not let you go, unless
you tell your Name to me;
with all your great salvation bless,
and make me all like you.

Then let me on the mountaintop
behold your open face;
where faith in sight is swallowed up,
and prayer in endless praise.

James Martineau

God eternal, in whose appointment our life stands, you have committed our work to us, and we would commit our cares to you. May we feel that we are not our own, and that you will heed our wants, while we are intent upon your will. May we never dwell carelessly or say in our hearts: "I am here, and there is no one over me," nor anxiously as though our path were hid.

But with a mind simply fixed upon our trust, and choosing nothing but the dispositions of your providence. More and more fill us with that pity for others' troubles, which comes from forgetfulness of our own, and the glad hope of the children of eternity. And to you, the beginning and the end, Lord of the living, refuge of the dying, be thanks and praise forever.

Short Memos to God

The grace of our Lord Jesus Christ, and the love of God, and the fellowship of the Holy Spirit be with us all, evermore. Amen.

—Traditional blessing on God's people

The *Book of Common Prayer*

Almighty God, Lord of heaven and earth: We humbly pray that your gracious providence may give and preserve to our use the harvests of the land and of the seas, and may prosper all who labor to gather them, that we, who constantly receive good things from your hand, may always give you thanks, through Jesus Christ our Lord, who lives and reigns with you and the Holy Spirit, one God, forever and ever. Amen.

At Our "Wit's End"

(Adapted from the writings of Mrs. Charles Cowman)

"They ... were at their wits' end. 'LORD, help!' they cried in their trouble, and he saved them from their distress." (Psalm 107:27–28)

Are you standing at "Wit's End Corner,"
Christian, with troubled brow?
Are you thinking of what is before you,
And all you are bearing now?
Does all the world seem against you,
And you in the battle alone?
Remember—at "Wit's End Corner"
Is just where God's power is shown.

Are you standing at "Wit's End Corner,"
Blinded with wearying pain,
Feeling you cannot endure it,
You cannot bear the strain,
Bruised through the constant suffering,
Dizzy, and dazed, and numb?
Remember—at "Wit's End Corner"
Is where Jesus loves to come.

Are you standing at "Wit's End Corner?"
Your work before you spread,
All lying begun, unfinished,
And pressing on heart and head,
Longing for strength to do it,
Stretching out trembling hands?
Remember—at "Wit's End Corner"
The Burden-bearer stands.

Are you standing at "Wit's End Corner?"
Then you're just in the very spot
To learn the wondrous resources

Of Him who fails not:
No doubt to a brighter pathway
Your footsteps will soon be moved,
But only at "Wit's End Corner"
Is the "God who is able" proved.

—Antoinette Wilson

Catherine of Siena

In mercy you have seen fit today to show me, poor as I am, how we can in no way pass judgment on other people's intentions. Indeed, by sending people along an endless variety of paths, you give me an example for myself, and for this I thank you.

James S. Bell Jr.

Loving Heavenly Father, thank you for your Holy Spirit who fills our hearts with a serene assurance that we belong to you forever. How wonderful to be a child of the great King over all the earth, a God of love who does not desire that any should perish. Take away doubts and fears when we become estranged to you or experience a dark night of the soul. When suffering strikes or injustice happens, let us not blame you but understand that all things inevitably work for the good for those who love God and are called according to his purpose. Grant us the things that lead to assurance—greater faith, greater trust, and greater hope. As we grow in assurance, then lead us to endurance, knowing that we can overcome any obstacle, including death itself.

Short Memos to God

Father, your Word tells us that you know what we need before we even ask. I thank you for the privilege of asking anyway.

—Tracy Macon Sumner

Saint Barnabas

Lord God almighty, out of your great charity, pour down upon us a spirit of tender love to you and a pitiful compassion toward all sufferers. In every difficulty be our guide, in temptation our defense, in weakness our strength, in weariness our rest, that, being transformed by your Spirit into the image of your holiness, we may finally attain to that blessed home of everlasting rest and joy, where you, Father, with the Son and the Holy Spirit, live and reign, one God forever and ever.

H. C. G. Moule

The blessing of the Lord rest and remain upon all his people, in every land and of every tongue. The Lord meet in mercy all who seek him; the Lord comfort all who suffer and mourn; the Lord hasten his coming, and give us his people peace by all means.

James S. Bell Jr.

Lord Jesus, as we recount our needs in prayer we remember that more than anything we need a savior. We thank you for so great a salvation, delivering us from eternal death and meeting all of our spiritual and material needs in what you did in the cross and resurrection. Your Word says that you will supply all our needs according to your riches in glory. Help us to know our true needs for holiness and the fruits of your Spirit. We also know that you are interested in our personal desires and for your name's sake answer those requests that you deem to be good for us. Let us use our gifts and talents to provide for ourselves, but help us to remember that you have given us the abilities themselves and we should never become independent of you.

Short Memos to God

Lord, we beg you, grant your people grace to withstand the temptations of the world, the flesh, and the devil, and with pure hearts and minds to follow thee, the only God.

—The *Gelasian Sacramentary*

The Narrow Way

O Lord Jesus, who came to be poor rather than rich, have mercy on all who are in need and want. Comfort them in all sorrows, supply their needs, raise up friends for them, and give them grace to learn of You, and always to put their trust in your help. Have mercy, blessed Savior, on all who are living in sin, all who pray not for themselves, and who care not for their own souls. Turn them to yourself, and teach them to look to the things which belong to their peace before they are hidden from their eyes.

Benjamin Jenks

As you make the outgoings of the morning and evening to rejoice, so lift up the light of your countenance upon us and make us glad with the tokens of your love. Be with us, Lord, and let your grace follow us today, and all the days of our lives. Be our guide until we die, in death our comfort, and after death our portion and happiness everlasting.

Robert Collyer

Father, this day may bring some hard task to our lives, or some hard trial to our love. We may grow weary, or sad, or hopeless in our lot. But, Father, our whole life until now has been on great proof of your care. Bread has come for our bodies, thoughts to our minds, love to our hearts, and all of these from you. So help us, we plead, while we stand still on this side of all that the day may bring, to resolve that we will trust you this day to shine into gloom of the mind, to stand by us in any trial of our love, and to give us rest in your good time as we need. May this day be full of power that shall bring us near to you, and make us more like you. And God, may we so trust you this day that when the day is done our trust shall be firmer than ever. Then, when our last day comes and our work is done, we may trust you in death and forever, in the spirit of Jesus Christ our Lord.

Prayer for Gifts and Grace

We humbly beg you, Lord, for the gifts and for the grace of the Holy Spirit. Give us more love for you and for our neighbors. Give us more joy in worship, more peace at all times, more long-suffering, gentleness, and kindness of heart and manner. May we know something of what it means to be filled with the Holy Spirit. For the sake of Jesus Christ our Lord. Amen.

Gottfried Arnold

Most merciful God and Father, we commit ourselves and all we have to your almighty hands and ask you to preserve us by your good Spirit from all sin, misfortune, and grief of heart. Give us the spirit of grace and prayer, that we may have consoling trust in your love and that our petitions may be acceptable in your sight. Give us the spirit of faith to kindle a bright flame of true and blessed faith in our hearts, that we may have a living knowledge of salvation, and our whole life may be a thank offering for the mercies we have received. Give us the spirit of love, that we may experience the sweetness of your love toward us, and also love you in return, and render our obedience, not from constraint like slaves, but with the willing and joyful hearts of children.

Tracy Macon Sumner

Father, you have promised me in your word to meet all my needs according to your glorious riches. Help me to always remember that promise and to depend on you to provide everything I need. Help me to remember that if I need it, I'll have it, and that if I don't have it, I don't need it.

Irish Prayer for God's Blessings

Bless this house, O Lord, we pray.
Make it safe by night and day.
Bless these walls so firm and stout,
Keeping want and trouble out.
Bless the roof and chimney tall,
Let thy peace lie over all.
Bless the doors that they may prove
Ever open to joy and love.
Bless the windows shining bright,
Letting in God's heavenly light.

Bless the hearth a-blazing there,
With smoke ascending like a prayer.
Bless the people here within,
Keep them pure and free from sin.
Bless us all, that one day, we
May be fit, O Lord, to dwell with thee.

Short Memos to God

Dear God, be good to me. The sea is so wide and my boat is so small.

—Irish fisherman's prayer

Jeremy Taylor

Relieve and comfort, Lord, all the persecuted and afflicted. Speak peace to troubled consciences, strengthen the weak, confirm the strong, instruct the ignorant, deliver the oppressed from him that oppresses him, and relieve the need that has no helper. Bring us all, by the waters of comfort and in the ways of righteousness, to the kingdom of rest and glory; through Jesus Christ our Lord.

Lancelot Andrewes

God of providence, grant to farmers and keepers of cattle good seasons; to the fleet and fishers fair weather; to tradesmen not to overreach one another; even down to the meanest workman, even down to the poor; for Christ's sake. Amen.

Hippolytus of Rome

We give thanks to you, almighty Lord God, for making us worthy to see the fruits which the earth has produced. Bless them, Lord, as the crown of the year, according to your love and kindness, and let them be for the satisfying of the poor among your people.

And bless your servants who have offered these first fruits out of your gifts, because they fear you. Bless them from your holy heaven, together with their households and their children, and pour upon them your mercy and your holy grace, that they may know your will in all things, and cause them to inherit that which is in heaven.

The Malabar Liturgy

Strengthen for your service Lord, the hands that have stretched out to receive your holy things, that they may daily bring forth a harvest of good works to your glory. Grant that the ears which have heard the sound of your songs may be closed to the voice of clamor and dispute, that the eyes which have seen your great love may behold the fulfill-ment they hope for, that the tongues which have sung your praises may ever speak the truth, that the feet which have trodden your courts may walk in the light, and that the bodies which have tasted your risen body may be restored to newness of life. And may your great love remain with us forever, so that we may return abundant praise to your majesty.

Prayer for Blessing

You know, heavenly Father, the duties that lie before us this day, the dangers that may confront us, the sins that most beset us. Guide us, strengthen us, protect us. Give us your life in such abundance that we may become a power for righteousness among our fellow men. Let us find your power, your love, your life in all mankind and thus may we know you our Father in heaven.

Short Memos to God

May God the Father bless us. May Christ take care of us; the Holy Spirit enlighten us all the days of our lives. The Lord be our defender and keeper of body and soul, now and forever, to the ages of ages.

—*The Book of Cerne*

Søren Kierkegaard

God of compassion: we know that every good gift and every perfect gift comes down from you, but you have not sent us into the world empty-handed. Grant that our hand might not be closed and that our heart not be hardened. Add yourself the blessing so that our gift might come from on high, from you, good and perfect Lord.

Traditional Celtic Blessing

May the blessing of light be on you,
Light without and light within.
May the blessed sunlight shine upon you and warm your heart
Till it glows like a great fire,
And strangers may warm themselves as well as friends.

And may the light shine out of the eyes of you
Like a candle set in the window of a house,
Bidding the wanderer to come in out of the storm.

May the blessing of rain be on you, the soft sweet rain. May it fall upon your spirit so that little flowers may spring up and shed their sweetness in the air.

And may the blessing of the great rains be on you, to beat upon your spirit and wash it fair and clean, and leave there a shining pool where the blue of heaven shines, and sometimes a star.

May the blessing of the earth be upon you, the great round earth. May you ever have a kindly greeting for people as you're going along the roads.

And now may the Lord bless you, and bless you kindly.
Amen.

Be Good to Me, Lord

(By Tracy Macon Sumner)

"Be good to your servant, that I may live and obey your word." (Psalm 119:17)

In Psalm 119, by far the longest of the 150 psalms, the psalmist goes to great lengths to talk about the goodness of God, of His word, and His law.

Early on in this psalm, he asks God to bless him so that he may be able to live and obey his word. At a glance it might look like he's saying that as long as God gives him what he wants and needs, then he will be obedient.

But a better reading of that verse tell us that the psalmist is acknowledging that it is only God's goodness and His willingness to bless His people that allows and enables him to obediently do the things God has set out for him to do.

In other words, this is a prayer of utter dependence on the goodness and generosity of God. This tells us something we need to lay hold of, namely that our God is not offended when we, with open hands and humble hearts, approach the His throne and humbly ask Him to give us the things we need to consistently obey His commands.

Andrew Bonar, the nineteenth-century Scottish preacher, acknowledged this when he wrote, "God's exceeding greatness, his sympathy in my sorrow, his marking every tear—all of these things underscore the immensity of his grace and compassion. Therefore I can plead, 'Be good to your servant, that I may live and obey your word!'"

Every part of God's goodness to us—all His blessings, physical and spiritual alike—is for the purpose of helping to enable us to obey the commands He has given us in His written Word, the Bible.

We serve a God who wants us to walk every day in obedience. But He's a God who never intended for us to "go it alone." On the contrary, He's a God who is more than willing to give us everything we need to live the lives He has called us to live.

Chapter 9

Prayers for Guidance and Direction

Who among us hasn't had times in our lives when we were faced with a big decision and needed the counsel and advice of a friend in order to make that decision?

Decisions in the believer's life involving careers, marriage, and other "biggies" are ones that our God is deeply concerned about, and He wants us to seek His direction about them.

In the Bible, God identifies Himself not only as a God who loves and cares for His people, but also one who guides and directs them in everyday matters. King David, for example, prayed to the God he knew as his director and guide: "Show me the path where I should walk, O Lord; point out the right road for me to follow. Lead me by your truth and teach me, for you are the God who saves me. All day long I put my hope in you." (Psalm 25:4–5)

David wasn't the first believer to ask God for direction and guidance. He was also far from the last. Here are some specially selected prayers seeking God's guidance and direction.

Rupert Mayer

Lord, what you will let it be so.
Where you will, there we will go.
What is your will? Help us to know.
Lord, when you will, the time is right.
In you there's joy in strife.
For Your will I'll give my life.

To ease your burden brings no pain.
To forego all for you is gain,
as long as I in you remain.

Because you will it, it is best.
Because you will it we are blest.
Till in your hands, our hearts find rest,
till in your hands, our hearts find rest.

Short Memos to God

Guide us, O Christ, in all the perplexities of our modern social life, and in your own good time bring us together in love and unity, making the kingdoms of this world your kingdom as you will.

—James Aderley

John Donne

Eternal and most glorious God: you alone steer my boat through all its voyages, but you have a more special care of it when it comes to a narrow current or to a dangerous fall of waters. You have a care of the preservation of my body in all the ways of my life; but, in the straits of death, open your eyes wider and enlarge your intervention toward me so far that no illness or agony may shake and numb the soul. Please make my bed in all my sickness so that, being used to your hand, I may be content with any bed of your making.

James S. Bell Jr.

Almighty and most merciful Father, we ask today that you would "be thou our vision" and guide and direct our steps in the way we should go. We are your sheep, the sheep of your pasture, and you have promised us you would lead in your paths of righteousness for your name's sake. Give us the ability to walk in the straight and narrow path that leads to life and peace. Keep us from presumption, ignorance, and deception as we seek you for guidance in all our decisions. Help us to use both the reason you have given us as well as the spiritual discernment that comes from above. You are a God who is concerned about the smallest details in our lives so help us to pray for your will in the small things, too.

Tracy Macon Sumner

Lord Jesus Christ, you have told us that the most important commandment is that I love you with all my heart, soul, mind, and strength and that I love my neighbor as myself. Lord, I ask you to lead me in loving my neighbor. Guide me toward those who today are in need of a gentle word or an act of kindness in your name. Help me to remember that in loving those you have created, I am also expressing my love for you today.

Short Memos to God

God be in my head, and in my understanding;
God be in my eyes, and in my looking;
God be in my mouth, and in my speaking;
God be in my heart, and in my thinking;
God be at my end, and at my departing.

—Sarum Primer

Christina Rossetti

Our God, bestow upon us such confidence, such peace, such happiness in you that your will may always be dearer to us than our own will, and your pleasure than our own pleasure. All that you give is your free gift to us, all that you take away is your grace to us. Be thanked for all, praised for all, loved for all, through Jesus Christ our Lord.

Ancient Prayer for Guidance

Almighty Lord our God, direct our steps this day into the way of peace, and strengthen our hearts to obey your commandments. May the Dayspring visit us from on high, and give light to those who sit in darkness and the shadow of death, that they may adore you for your mercy, follow you for your truth, desire you for your sweetness, you who are the blessed Lord God of Israel, both now and evermore.

God, Our Loving Shepherd-Father

(By Tracy Macon Sumner; based on Psalm 23, a Psalm of David)

1. The LORD is my shepherd; I have everything I need.

When God guides as our Shepherd-Father, we don't need anything else, because He is leading us from a position of perfect love, knowledge, and wisdom.

2. He lets me rest in green meadows; he leads me beside peaceful streams.

Even in the busiest and most hectic of times, God gives us perfect peace and rest just because we know and trust Him.

3. He renews my strength. He guides me along right paths, bringing honor to his name.

It's one thing to guide and direct someone, but it's completely another to give that person the strength to get through whatever his or her path brings along. Our Shepherd-Father does both!

4. Even when I walk through the dark valley of death, I will not be afraid, for you are close beside me. Your rod and your staff protect and comfort me.

God never promised His people a life free from worry or trials, but He promises that He will be with us as we follow His leading. That means in all situations, even ones that are unpleasant or even dangerous. For that reason, we don't need to fear anything.

5. You prepare a feast for me in the presence of my enemies. You welcome me as a guest, anointing my head with oil. My cup overflows with blessings.

Putting your faith and trust in a Father-Shepherd ensures that your life here on Earth will be blessed because He directs and guides everything that happens to and for you.

6. Surely your goodness and unfailing love will pursue me all the days of my life, and I will live in the house of the LORD forever.

Not only are we ensured of God's love and guidance in this life, but we are also promised a place in His eternal kingdom.

Thomas Aquinas

O creator past all telling, you have appointed from the treasures of your wisdom the hierarchies of angels, disposing them in wondrous order above the bright heavens, and have so beautifully set out all parts of the universe.

You we call the true fount of wisdom and the noble origin of all things. Be pleased to shed on the darkness of mind in which I was born, the twofold beam of your light and warmth to dispel my ignorance and sin.

You make eloquent the tongues of children. Then instruct my speech and touch my lips with graciousness. Make me keen to understand, quick to learn, able to remember; make me delicate to interpret and ready to speak.

Guide my going in and going forward, lead home my going forth. You are true God and true man, and live forever and ever.

Short Memos to God

You alone know best what is good for me. As I am not my own but completely yours, so neither do I desire that my will be done, but yours, nor will I have any will but yours.

—Francis Borgia

Tracy Macon Sumner

Thank you, Lord, for teaching me that there is no place in life more fulfilling or comfortable or joyful than that place in which I am doing what I know you want me to do. Guide and direct me to that place, and help me always to listen for your voice and do follow your leading not only when it comes to the "bigger picture" of my life, but also in even the smallest things I do daily.

Workday Prayer (Author Unknown)

Lord Jesus, as I enter this workplace, I bring your presence with me. I speak your peace, your grace, and your perfect order into the atmosphere of this office. I acknowledge your Lordship over all that will be spoken, thought, decided and accomplished within these walls.

Lord Jesus, I thank you for the gifts you have deposited in me. I do not take them lightly, but commit to using them responsibly and well. Give me a fresh supply of truth and beauty on which to draw as I do my job.

Anoint my creativity, my ideas, my energy so that even my smallest task may bring you honor. Lord, when I am confused, guide me. When I am weary, energize me. Lord, when I am burned out, infuse me with the light of your Holy Spirit.

May the work that I do and the way I do it bring hope, life, and courage to all that I come in contact with today. And oh Lord, even in this day's most stressful moment, may I rest in you.

✦ Short Memos to God

Lord Jesus Christ, who alone is perfect wisdom, you know what is best for us. Mercifully grant that it may happen to us only as it pleases you and seems good in your sight today.

—King Henry VI

George Dawson

Almighty God, we bless and praise you that we have wakened to the light of another earthly day. And now we will think of what a day should be.

Our days are yours, so let them be spent for you. Our days are few, so let them be spent with care. We ask you to shine on this day—the day which we may call our own.

Lord, as we go to our daily work, help us to take pleasure in it. Show us clearly what our duty is and help us to be faithful in doing it. Let all we do be well done, fit for your eye to see. Give us strength to do, patience to bear; let our courage never fail.

When we cannot love our work, let us think of it as your task, and by our true love to you make unlovely things shine in the light of your great love.

Short Memos to God

Grant that I may love you always, then do with me as you will.

—Ignatius of Loyola

Thomas Wilson

Lord, make your way plain before our face. Support us this day under all the difficulties we shall meet with. We offer ourselves to you, God, this day to do in us and with us as to seems best to you, through Jesus Christ our Lord.

Saint Jerome

Lord, you have given us your Word for a light to shine upon our path. Grant us so to meditate on that Word, and to follow its teaching that we may find in it the light that shines more and more until the perfect day, through Jesus Christ our Lord.

William Bright

God, grant us in all our doubts and uncertainties the grace to ask what you would have us do. Grant that the spirit of wisdom may save us from all wrong choices and that in your light we may see light, and in your straight path we may not stumble, through Jesus Christ our Lord.

Francis of Assisi

God almighty, eternal, righteous, and merciful, give to us poor sinners to do for your sake all that we know of your will, and to will always what pleases you, so that inwardly purified, enlightened, and kindled by the fire of your Holy Spirit, we may follow in the footprints of your well-beloved Son, our Lord Jesus Christ.

 **Short Memos to God**

Glorious God, enlighten the darkness of our minds. Give us a right faith, a firm hope, and a perfect love, so that we may always and in all things act according to your perfect will.

—Francis of Assisi

Teresa of Avila

Govern everything by your wisdom, Lord, so that my soul may always be serving you as you choose, not as I choose. Do not punish me, I implore you, by granting that which I wish or ask, if it offend your love, which would always live in me. Let me die to myself that so I may serve you. Let me live to you who in yourself are the true life.

Thomas Wilson

Heavenly Father, subdue in me whatever is contrary to your holy will. Grant that I may always study to know your will, so that I may know how to please you. Grant, my God, that I may never run into those temptations which, in my prayers, I desire to avoid. Lord, never permit my trials to be above my strength.

Tracy Macon Sumner

Lord, sometimes it's hard to hear your voice through all the noise of everyday life. I pray that you will make your leading and direction in my life so clear and understandable that I can hear and see it clearly, then do it, knowing that you have my very best and, more important, your glory in mind in all that you have me do every day.

Jeremy Taylor

Guide us, Lord, in all the changes and varieties of the world, so that we may have evenness and tranquility of spirit, that we may not murmur in adversity nor in prosperity wax proud, but in serene faith resign our souls to your most holy will.

Short Memos to God

Lord, I am blind and helpless, stupid and ignorant. Cause me to hear. Cause me to know. Teach me to do. Lead me.

—Henry Martyn

Hannah Whitall Smith

Lord Jesus, I believe that you are able and willing to deliver me from all the care and unrest and bondage of my Christian life. I believe you did die to set me free, not only in the future, but now and here. I believe you are stronger than sin, and that you can keep me, even me, in my extreme of weakness, from falling in its snares or yielding obedience to its commands. And Lord, I am going to trust you to keep me. I have tried keeping myself, and have failed, and failed most grievously. I am absolutely helpless. So now I will trust you. I give myself to you. I keep back no reserves. Body, soul, and spirit, I present myself to you as a piece of clay, to be fashioned into anything your love and your wisdom shall choose. And now I am yours. I believe you do accept that which I present to you; I believe that this poor, weak, foolish heart has been taken possession of by you; and that you have even at this very moment begun to work in me to will and to do of your good pleasure. I trust you utterly, and trust you now.

Short Memos to God

Naked I came from my mother's womb, and naked I will depart. The Lord gave and the Lord has taken away; may the name of the Lord be praised.

—Job's Prayer (Job 1:21)

Anglican Prayer for Guidance

Eternal God and Father, by whose power we are created and by whose love we are redeemed: guide and strengthen us by your Spirit, that we may give ourselves to your service, and live this day in love to one another and to you; through Jesus Christ our Lord. Amen.

Celtic Prayer for Guidance

O God, listen to my prayer
Let my earnest petition come to you,
for I know that you are hearing me
As surely as though I saw you with mine eyes.

I am placing a lock upon my heart,
I am placing a lock upon my thoughts,
I am placing a lock upon my lips
And double-knitting them.

Aught that is amiss for my soul
In the pulsing of my death,
May you, O God, sweep it from me
And may you shield me in the blood of your love.

Let no thought come to my heart,
Let no sound come to my ear,
Let no temptation come to my eye,
Let no fragrance come to my nose,
Let no fancy come to my mind,
Let no ruffle come to my spirit,
That is hurtful to my poor body this night,
Nor ill for my soul at the hour of my death;

But may you yourself, O God of life,
Be at my breast, be at my back,
You to me as a star, you to me as a guide,
From my life's beginning to my life's closing.

When God's Directions Don't Make Sense

(By Tracy Macon Sumner)

"The Lord gave this message to Jonah son of Amittai: 'Get up and go the great city of Nineveh! Announce my judgment against it because I have seen how wicked its people are.'" (Jonah 1:1, 2)

Jonah had received God's instructions, and they couldn't have been any clearer. He was to go to a city called Nineveh and warn them that their wicked ways were about to bring God's wrath if they didn't repent.

Jonah heard God clearly, but he just couldn't understand why he was being asked to go to such a place. Jonah's real problem with being sent to Nineveh was that it was inhabited by those who were fierce enemies of Jonah's own people. So Jonah did what so many people do when they are told to do something that doesn't make sense: he ran the other way. He boarded a ship and sailed for a place called Tarshish, which was in exactly the opposite direction of Nineveh.

It wasn't long before God caught up with Jonah. As he rested in the ship, a huge storm arose and threatened to sink it. So instead of going down with the ship, Jonah told the captain that he was the reason God had raised up the storm and to just toss him over-board.

If you attended Sunday school class as a child, you know by now that Jonah didn't just drown but was instead swallowed by a huge fish. As he spent three days in the fish's belly, he repented and finally agreed to go to Nineveh, as God had directed him in the first place.

Jonah's story shows us that sometimes God's leads, guides, or directs us to do things that don't make human sense—things like extending love to the most unlovable or telling someone who doesn't seem to want to hear about God at all about the love extended him or her through Jesus Christ.

When God directs you to do something that just doesn't make sense, don't hesitate to obey. It just might be that He's trying to extend His love and compassion to someone you wouldn't have expected.

Part 3

"Difference-Making" Prayers

The Christian faith is one that is supposed to empower us to make changes—in ourselves and in the world around us. The next four chapters deal with the kinds of prayers that help us to make both inner changes and outward changes. These are prayers asking God for strength, transformed character, the ability to be content in him, and for those who desire to serve others in the name of Jesus Christ. Read these prayers and find out the ways in which God wants to change us, use us, and cause us to live just like Jesus lived.

Chapter 10

Prayers for Strength in Spiritual Battle

As you read through the Bible, you find that the Christian faith isn't for the faint of heart or for those without courage. On the contrary, it is likened to a war—a spiritual war in which the devil will do everything he can to sidetrack us in our faith.

That sounds pretty ominous, doesn't it? But the good news is that God has given us every weapon we need to fight off the devil's attacks. This is what the Apostle Paul called the "full armor of God." (Ephesians 6:11) Here is what Paul said about that armor and how we can use it:

"Stand your ground, putting on the sturdy belt of truth and the body armor of God's righteousness. For shoes, put on the peace that comes from the Good News, so that you will be fully prepared. In every battle you will need faith as your shield to stop the fiery arrows aimed at you by Satan. Put on salvation as your helmet, and take the sword of the Spirit, which is the word of God. Pray at all times and on every occasion in the power of the Holy Spirit." (Ephesians 6:14–18)

This passage tells us several things about being strong through the power of God. First, it likens our spiritual lives to a war—war in which we will need to use every weapon at our disposal to fight off the advances of the devil. Second, it tells us that God has already given us every weapon we need in order to win that war. Third, it lays out in detail what those weapons are and what they do. Fourth, it tells us that being in constant prayer is the key to making effective use of those weapons.

This chapter is made up of prayers that relate to this spiritual battle. God never promised it would be easy, but He has promised to give us what we need to win. The bottom line? What we need is Him!

King David

The Lord is my light and my salvation—so why should I be afraid? The Lord protects me from danger—so why should I tremble? When evil people come to destroy me, when my enemies and foes attack me, they will stumble and fall. Though a mighty army surrounds me, my heart will know no fear. Even if they attack me, I remain confident. (Psalm 27:1–3)

Short Memos to God

Grant that I may not pray alone with the mouth; help me that I may pray from the depths of my heart.
—Martin Luther

Benjamin Jenks

Not only lay your commands on us, Lord, but be pleased to enable us to perform every duty you require of us. Make our hearts so engaged with you that we make it our food and drink to do your will and wholeheartedly live according to your commands. Be merciful to us, bless us, and keep us this day in everything we do. Let your love flourish in our hearts and sweetly and powerfully keep us in faithful and cheerful obedience.

Wilfred Hornby

Our Lord, who sent your angel to purge Isaiah's lips with a burning coal from the altar so that he could be free to preach your Word to the people, whether or not they would hear: give your ministers and people pure and wise hearts, that so they would desire to go wherever you send them and do your will—both in the power of him through whom we do all things, your Son Jesus Christ our Lord.

James Martineau

Almighty God, who has created us in your own image, grant us grace to fearlessly challenge evil and to make no peace with oppression. That we may reverently use our freedom, help us to employ it in the upholding of justice in our communities and throughout the world. All this to glorify your holy name and through Jesus Christ our Lord, who lives and rules with you and the Holy Spirit—one God, now, and forever.

 **Short Memos to God**

Lord, give your servants patience to be still and hear your will, courage to venture wholly on your arm that will not harm, the wisdom that will never let us stray out of our way.

—John Mason Neale

Christina Rossetti

Lord God, whose strength is sufficient for all who lay hold of it, allow that in you we may be comforted in heart and strong. Grant us humility, meekness, temperance, purity, large heartedness, sympathy, and zeal—all of which are evidence of faith, handmaids of hope, and fruits of love. All this for the sake of Jesus Christ, our strength, our righteousness, and our hope of glory.

John Calvin

Grant, almighty God, as you shine on us through your word that we may not be blind at midnight nor intentionally seek darkness and thus lull ourselves to sleep. Instead, may we be awakened daily by your words. May we stir up ourselves more and more to fear your name and thus present ourselves and all our pursuits as a sacrifice to you so that you may rule in us peaceably and perpetually dwell in us until that time when you gather us to your heavenly home, where you have reserved for us rest and glory through Jesus Christ our Lord.

Arthur Henry McCheane

Most merciful Lord, we humbly request that you will give courage to your soldiers, wisdom to the confused, endurance to those who suffer, fresh energy and interest in life to those who have lost heart, a sense of your presence to the lonely, and blessing and prosperity to this household, for the sake of Jesus Christ.

Jeremy Taylor

Lord, I humbly ask you to visit this habitation with your mercy and me with your grace and salvation. Let your holy angels pitch their tents round about and dwell here so that no illusion of the night may abuse me, so that the spirits of darkness may not come near to hurt me, so that no evil or sad accident oppress me. And let the eternal Spirit of the Father dwell in my soul and body, filling every corner of my heart with light and grace. Let no deed of darkness overtake me. Let your blessing, most blessed God, be upon me forever, through Christ our Lord.

Augustine of Hippo

Breath in me, Holy Spirit, that my thoughts may all be holy. Act in me, Holy Spirit, that my work, too, may be holy. Draw my heart, Holy Spirit, that I love but what is holy. Strengthen me, Holy Spirit, to defend all that is holy. Guard me, then, Holy Spirit, that I always may be holy.

George Dawson

Lord, fill us so completely with your spirit that we, as we go from one thing to another, may go from strength to strength, always filled with your praise, everywhere filled with your work, finding the joy of the Lord to be our strength. This until the time when the work of this world is finished, the weary hours come to an end, and darkness shall come, and our eyes shall rest for awhile. Then give us an abundant entrance into eternal life, through Jesus Christ our Lord.

Tracy Macon Sumner

Father, you have shown me that your Word is profitable to me in every area of my walk with you as well as in my relationships with those you call my neighbors. But you have also shown me that it is a powerful weapon against the schemes of the devil. I pray that I may constantly follow the example of your Son who simply answered, "It is written" when the enemy tempted him. Remind me daily and in every temptation that your Word has power over the enemy and over his every tactic against me.

Short Memos to God

God bless this church and parish, and prosper all our attempts to be faithful and to draw others to you, for Jesus Christ's sake.

—Old Scottish prayer

The *Gelasian Sacramentary*

Almighty and everlasting God, who has revealed your glory by Christ among all nations, continue the work of your mercy so that your church, which is spread throughout the world, may continue with unwavering faith in confession of your name, through Jesus Christ our Lord.

Put on the Whole *Armor*

(Adapted from the writings of Matthew Henry; based on Ephesians 6:10–18)

During times of spiritual warfare and suffering, we need spiritual strength and courage, and if we want all of God's blessings during those times, we must make sure we put on *all* of God's armor and keep it on at all times.

Paul uses word pictures of a well-armored and armed solder in this passage, and each part of the armor is effective in warding off the enemy's fiercest frontal assaults.

◆ **Truth,** or sincerity, is the belt (verse 14). Every other piece of armor is dependent on the belt. We can have no spiritual victory unless we cling to God's truth.

◆ **God's righteousness,** which He accredits us through Christ, is the body armor (verse 14), which protects our hearts against a frontal attack.

◆ **The Good News of the Gospel** (verse 15) is the shoes in the full armor, and that tells us that we are to march forward, even in the midst of the worst trials, and battle the enemy.

◆ **Faith,** which means relying on what we can't see, is to be our shield (verse 16) to stop the fiery darts of temptation and deception the devil aims at us.

◆ **Salvation** is to be our helmet (verse 17), and that means maintaining the hope and assurance of the ultimate, eternal victory over the devil.

Paul mentions only one weapon of offense: the *sword of the Spirit*, or the Word of God (verse 17). That is plenty when it comes to going on the offensive against the devil. The truth of scripture can defeat our enemy.

Prayer (verse 18) must hold together all the other parts of God's armor. We must engage in all kinds of prayer: public, private, secret, and we must include all parts of prayer, including confession, requests for mercy, and thanksgiving.

Eugène Bersier

God, you know our hearts, and you see our temptations and struggles. Have pity on us and deliver us from the sins which make war upon our souls. You are all-powerful, and we are weak and erring. Faithful God, our trust is in you. Deliver us from the bondage of evil, and grant that we may from now on be your devoted servants, serving you in the freedom of holy love, for Jesus Christ's sake.

Short Memos to God

Almighty God, we humbly ask you to help those whose trust is under the shadow of your wings may, through the help of your power, overcome all evils that rise up against us.

—The Roman Breviary

Thomas Aquinas

Give us, Lord, a steadfast heart, one which no unworthy affection may drag down. Give us an unconquered heart, one which no difficulty can wear out. Give us an upright heart, one which no unworthy purpose may tempt into moving aside. Lord our God, give upon us also understanding to know you, diligence to seek you, wisdom to find you, and faithfulness that may finally embrace you, through Jesus Christ our Lord.

The Venerable Bede

May your Spirit, Christ, lead me in the right way, keeping me safe from all evil and destruction. And, being free from all malice, may I search diligently your holy Word to discover with the eyes of my mind your commandments. Finally, give me the strength of will to put those commandments into practice through every day of my life.

***

My God, who is the only hope of the world and the only refuge for unhappy men, who abides in the faithfulness of heaven: give me strong assistance in this place of testing. King, protect your man from absolute ruin, lest the one weak in faith surrender to the tyrant and face innumerable blows alone. Remember as I am dust, wind, and shadow, and my life is as fleeting as the flower of grass. But may the eternal mercy which has shone from time of old rescue his servant from the jaws of the lion. You who came from on high in the cloak of flesh, strike down the dragon with that two-edged sword, so that our mortal flesh can war with the winds and beat down strongholds with our captain God.

Short Memos to God

Lord, we humbly ask you to give your people grace to withstand the temptations of the world, the flesh and the devil, and to do it with pure hearts and minds to follow you.
—The *Gelasian Sacramentary*

The *Book of Common Prayer*

Blessed Lord, who has caused all holy Scriptures to be written for our learning: grant that we may in such wise hear them, read, mark, learn, and inwardly digest them, that by patience and comfort of your holy Word, we may embrace, and ever hold fast the blessed hope of everlasting life, which you have given us in our Savior Jesus Christ.

Tracy Macon Sumner

Lord, I thank you that you have given me all the spiritual weapons I need not just to defend myself from the attacks of the devil, but also to go on the offensive against him daily. I pray that you will keep me ever mindful of the power I have in you and from you, and that you will show me new ways to use that power.

Edmund Grindal

We know, Lord, our weaknesses and how easily we can fall from you. Therefore, don't allow Satan to show his power and hatred for us, for we are not able to withstand his assaults. Always arm us, Lord, with your grace, and assist us with the Holy Spirit in all kinds of temptations, through Jesus Christ our Lord.

Short Memos to God

O Lord, I do not pray for tasks equal to my strength. I ask for strength equal to my tasks.
—Philips Brooks

Joseph Scriven

What a friend we have in Jesus,
all our sins and griefs to bear!
What a privilege to carry
everything to God in prayer!

O what peace we often forfeit,
O what needless pain we bear,
all because we do not carry
everything to God in prayer.

Have we trials and temptations?
Is there trouble anywhere?
We should never be discouraged;
take it to the Lord in prayer.

Can we find a friend so faithful
who will all our sorrows share?
Jesus knows our every weakness;
take it to the Lord in prayer.

Are we weak and heavy laden,
cumbered with a load of care?
Precious Savior, still our refuge;
take it to the Lord in prayer.

Do thy friends despise, forsake thee?
Take it to the Lord in prayer!
In his arms he'll take and shield thee;
thou wilt find a solace there.

 **Short Memos to God**

Almighty and everlasting God, who controls all things in heaven and earth, mercifully hear the requests of your people, and grant us your peace all the days of our lives.

—The *Gregorian Sacramentary*

William Edwin Orchard

Our God, we don't ask you to take us out of this life but to prove your power within it. We don't ask for tasks more suited to our strength, but for strength more suited to our tasks. Give us a vision that moves, the strength that endures, and the grace of Jesus Christ, who wore our flesh like a monarch's robe and walked our earthly life like a conqueror in triumph.

James S. Bell Jr.

Lord, help us not to forget that we are in a battle with enemies in the heavenly places, and we don't wage war with human weapons but with the weapons of the Spirit. Let us put on the armor of light, depending on your might power to make the enemy flee from us. We thank you that you have given us this authority through the precious blood of the Lamb and in the powerful name of Jesus we can overcome all spiritual opposition. We have your promise that if we resist the devil he will flee from us. Keep us from opening ourselves to his influence by allowing temptation to turn into sin. Help us to repent of any sinful habits that create strongholds for the enemy. May we examine our hearts by the inspiration of your Holy Spirit.

Prayer for Courage (Author Unknown)

God, make me brave for life: oh, braver than this. Let me straighten after pain, as a tree straightens after the rain, shining and lovely again.

God, make me brave for life; much braver than this. As the blown grass lifts, let me rise from sorrow with quiet eyes, knowing your way is wise.

God, make me brave; life brings such blinding things. Help me to keep my sight. Help me to see the fact that out of dark comes light.

Short Memos to God

Lord, grant us grace not only to be hearers of the word, but also doers of the same; not only to love, but to live your gospel; not only to profess, but also to practice your blessed commandments.

—Thomas Becon

Isaac Watts

Give me the wings of faith to rise within the veil, and see the saints above, how great their joys, how bright their glories be. Once they were mourning here below, their couch was wet with tears; they wrestled hard, as we do now, with sins and doubts and fears.

We ask them whence their victory came: they, with united breath, ascribe their conquest to the Lamb, their triumph to his death. They marked the footsteps that he trod, his zeal inspired their breast, and, following their incarnate God, possess the promised rest.

Our glorious leader claims our praise for his own pattern given; while the long cloud of witnesses show the same path to heaven.

Take Up Your Helmet and Sword

(Adapted from the writings of John Wesley)

"Put on salvation as your helmet, and take the sword of the Spirit, which is the word of God. Pray at all times and in the power of the Holy Spirit." (Ephesians 6:17–18)

Put on salvation as your helmet (also see 1 Thessalonians 5:8): in battle, the warrior's head is the part of his body that needs to be most carefully defended—a head wound very often proves to be fatal. The "spiritual armor" for our heads is our assurance of salvation. At the very least, this hope is a confidence that God will complete the work of faith within us; at the very best, it is the full assurance of future glory in heaven, which we can have because of our experiential knowledge of God's pardoning love. Armed with the helmet of salvation, Jesus Christ himself was "willing to die a shameful death on the cross because of the joy he knew would be his afterward." (Hebrews 12:2)

And take the sword of the Spirit, which is the word of God: if there is one thing Satan cannot withstand, it's when the believer wields the sword of God's Word wielded in faith. In the "armor of God" passage of Ephesians 6, all the armor listed prior to the second half of verse 17 is for defensive purposes. In referring to God's written Word as a sword, the Apostle Paul is telling us that we are not only to defend ourselves against the devil, but also to go on the offensive against him, with shield in one hand and the sword in the other. Whoever fights with the powers of hell will need the sword of the Spirit. Whoever is covered head to foot with armor but neglects the Word will be defeated after all.

This tells us one of the greatest things about being a Christian. And it tells us that we need to be complete in our faith and lacking nothing when it comes to standing against the devil.

God wants us to put on His whole armor, but there is one thing He wants just as much, if not more, and it's prayer.

Pray at all times and in the power of the Holy Spirit: God wants us praying "at all times," meaning in every occasion and situation, in the midst of all we do. That means praying inwardly through all things. And He wants us to do so under the influence of the Holy Spirit, who the Bible says will teach us how to pray.

Chapter 11

Prayers for Christ-Like Character

The Bible, especially the New Testament, is filled with commands and encouragements for the believer to walk, talk, and live in the same way Jesus did when he was alive on Earth. This is what Christians call "Christlikeness."

As we read of Jesus' words and deeds in the gospels, we can see that Christlikeness means a lot of things. It means living a life of love and compassion for our fellow humans, and it means being so concerned for their spiritual well-being that we take action. It also means caring for the sick, homeless, and hungry—just like Jesus did. And it means being devoted to doing the will of God in every area of our lives.

The Apostle Paul, writing to the church in Ephesus, a Greek city located in what is now Turkey, told believers:

"Follow God's example in everything you do, because you are his dear children. Live a life filled with love for others, following the example of Christ, who loved you and gave himself as a sacrifice to take away your sins. And God was pleased, because that sacrifice was like sweet perfume to him." (Ephesians 5:1–2)

While he walked the earth, Jesus himself told his disciples, "let your good deeds shine out for all to see, so that everyone will praise your heavenly Father." (Matthew 5:16) Jesus' point in saying that was simply that he wanted people to be able to see something different in the life of the believer. He wanted those who followed him to demonstrate the same kind of love, compassion, and devotion to God that he showed every day of his life on earth.

This has been the subject of more prayers and writings than we could fit in this book, some of which have survived for literally thousands of years. Here are some of those prayers and writings.

Mother Teresa of Calcutta

Lord, help us to see in your crucifixion and resurrection an example of how to endure and seemingly to die in the agony and conflict of daily life, so that we may live more fully and creatively. You accepted patiently and humbly the rebuffs of human life, as well as the tortures of your crucifixion and passion. Help us to accept the pains and conflicts that come to us each day as opportunities to grow as people and become more like you. Enable us to go through them patiently and bravely, trusting that you will support us. Make us realize that it is only by frequent deaths of ourselves and our self-centered desires that we can come to live more fully; for it is only by dying with you that we can rise with you.

Short Memos to God

Lord, I am willing to receive what you give, to lack what you withhold, to relinquish what you take, to suffer what you inflict, to be what you require.
—Charles Swindoll

Charles de Foucauld

Poverty, humility, penance—you, dear Jesus, know that I long to practice those virtues to the degree and in the way which you want. But what are the ways and the degrees? Until now I have always thought that I should practice them by imitating you as closely as possible, by making myself follow, as far as I could, the way in which you yourself practiced them. Yet, if I look at myself, there is such a gap between my wretchedness and true perfection, that I am certainly unworthy to be counted among those close disciples who tread in your footsteps. And yet you have heaped so many blessings on me that it would seem ungrateful not to strive for perfection. To be content with imperfection would seem like a rejection of your generosity. I find it hard to believe that, in giving yourself so freely to me, you do not want me to give myself wholly to you. My only desire is to be and to do what pleases you. Enlighten my mind that I may always conform to your will.

Short Memos to God

Our Father, change us, day by day, by the work of your Holy Spirit so that we may grow more like Christ in all that we think and say and do, to his glory.

—Søren Kierkegaard

Charles Kingsley

God, grant that looking upon the face of the Lord, as into a glass, we may be changed into his likeness from glory to glory. Take out of us all pride and vanity, boasting and forwardness; and give us the true courage which shows itself by gentleness; the true wisdom which shows itself by simplicity; and the true power which shows itself by modesty.

Tracy Macon Sumner

Jesus, when I have to deal with those who need you, help me to talk to them the way you did. When I meet those who are hurting and in need of a kind word or deed, help me to reach out to them, just like you did. When I see injustice or unrighteousness, help me to see it the way you did and to confront it, just like you did. When I have a decision to make, remind me to go to the Father and talk to him about it, just like you did. When I am mistreated or spoken ill of, help me to respond to it without offering "an eye for an eye," just like you did.

John Henry Newman

Stay with me, and then I shall begin to shine as you shine, to be a light to others. The light, Jesus, will be all from you. None of it will be mine. No merit belongs to me. It will be you who shines through me upon others. Let me praise you, in the way which you love best, by shining on all those around me. Give light to them as well as to me; bring light to them through me. Teach me to show forth your praise, your truth, your will. Make me preach you without preaching—not by words but by my example and by the sympathetic influence, of what I do—by my visible resemblance to your saints, and the evident fullness of love which my heart bears to you.

Short Memos to God

Lord, take our minds and think through them; take our lips and speak through them; take our lives and live out your life; take our hearts and set them on fire with love for you.
—William H. M. H. Aitken

James S. Bell Jr.

Grant most precious God that we may do everything according to your Word in the Book of Philippians where you ask us not to complain or argue but to become blameless and pure, children of God without fault in a wayward generation, in which we may shine like stars in the universe as we hold out to others the words of life. The Apostle Peter talks about the character process when he states that our faith should lead first to moral excellence, and then to self-control, patient endurance, and godliness. Lord, let that in turn lead to genuine love for others, the final character builder. Without these things we are short-sighted and blind to our character flaws. Give us the grace to bear the fruit of your Spirit, to be especially full of love, joy, peace, and patience.

Ashton Oxenden

Lord, your Word is before us, give us a meek and a reverent and teachable mind, while we read and study it. Blessed Spirit of God, be our teacher. Shine, Lord, upon your own sacred page and make it clear to us. What we do not see, show us, and where we are wrong, correct us. Bring home some portion of truth to our soul, and thus make us wise to salvation, through Jesus Christ our Savior."

━━━━◁◯◁ **Short Memos to God** ━━━━

Lord, give us the true courage that shows itself by gentleness; the true wisdom that shows itself by simplicity; and the true power that shows itself by modesty.

—Charles Kingsley

Henry Martyn

Send forth your light and your truth, that we may always live near you, our God. Let us feel your love, that we may be, as it were, already in heaven, that we may do our work as the angels do theirs; and let us be ready for every work, ready to go out or in, to stay or to depart, just as you direct. Lord, let us have no will of our own, or consider our true happiness as depending in the smallest degree on anything that happens to us outwardly, but as consisting totally in conformity to your will.

John Wesley

Jesus, poor, unknown, and despised, have mercy on us, and let us not be ashamed to follow you. Jesus, accused, and wrongfully condemned, teach us to bear insults patiently, and let us not seek our own glory. Jesus, crowned with thorns and hailed in derision; buffeted, overwhelmed with injuries, griefs and humiliations; Jesus, hanging on the accursed tree, bowing the head, giving up the ghost, have mercy on us, and conform our whole lives to your spirit. Amen.

━━━━◁◯◁ **Short Memos to God** ━━━━

Write upon our hearts, Lord God, the lessons of your holy word, and grant that we may all be doers of the same, and not forgetful hearers only.

—Alexander Campbell Fraser

Matthew Henry

Lord, lift up the light of your countenance upon us; let peace rule in our hearts, and may it be our strength and our song, throughout our pilgrimage. We commit ourselves to your care and keeping this day. Let your grace be mighty in us, and sufficient for us, and let it work in us both to will and to do of your own good pleasure, and grant us strength for all the duties of the day. Keep us from sin. Help us rule over our own spirits, and keep us from speaking unadvisedly with our words. May we live together in peace and holy love, and do command your blessing upon us, which is eternal life. Prepare us for all the events of the day, for we don't know what a day may bring forth. Give us grace to deny ourselves; to take up our cross daily, and to follow in the steps of our Lord and Master, Jesus Christ our Lord. Amen.

Henry Hammond

Holy Jesus, who came down from heaven and was pleased to pay the ransom on the cross for us, on purpose that you might redeem us from all sin, and purify to yourself a precious people, zealous for good works, we ask you to write your law on our hearts that we may understand it, that we may know you, and the power of your resurrection, and express it in turning from our sinful ways, that you may rule in our hearts by faith, and that we, being dead to sin and living rightly, may bear fruit leading to holiness, may grow in grace, and in the practical knowledge of you. Amen

Francis Bacon

Eternal and most merciful Father of Jesus Christ, through whom you have made a covenant of grace and mercy with all those that come to you through him: don't hold back the course of your mercies and loving-kindness toward us, but continually guide our feet in the paths of your right living and in the ways of your commandments, that through your grace we may be enabled to lead a godly, holy, sober, and Christian life in true sincerity and uprightness of heart before you, Lord, not for any merits of ours, but only for the merits of your Son, our Savior Jesus Christ.

Emulating Jesus' Character

(Adapted from the writings of Andrew Murray)

"Your attitude should be the same that Christ Jesus had." (Philippians 2:5)

In this view it is of tremendous importance that we should have right thoughts of who Christ is, of what really constitutes him, and especially of what may be counted as his chief characteristic, the root and essence of all his character as our Redeemer.

There can be but one answer: it is his humility. What is the incarnation but his heavenly humility, his emptying himself and becoming man? What is his life on earth but humility; his taking the form of a servant? And what is his redeeming work but humility! "He obediently humbled himself even further by dying a criminal's death on a cross." And what is his ascension and his glory, but humility exalted to the throne and crowned with glory? "Because of this, God raised him up to the heights of heaven." In heaven, where he was with the Father, in his birth, in his life, in his death, in his sitting on the throne, it is nothing but humility.

Christ is the humility of God embodied in human nature; the Eternal Love humbling itself, clothing itself in the garb of meekness and gentleness, to win and serve and save us. As the love and condescension of God makes him the benefactor and helper and servant of all, so Jesus of necessity was the Incarnate Humility. He still reigns in the midst of the throne, the meek and lowly Lamb of God.

Simon Patrick

Almighty and most merciful Father, in you we live and move and have our being. From you we have received tender mercy and compassion. To you we owe our safety in days past, together with all the comforts of this present life and the hopes of the life to come. We praise you, O God, our creator; to you we give our thanks, for you are our joy and crown. You daily pour out your good gifts upon us.

We humbly pray that Jesus our Lord, the hope of glory, may be more fully formed in us and evidenced in a growing humility, meekness, patience, contentment and absolute surrender of our whole lives—body, soul, and spirit—to your will and pleasure.

Do not leave us or forsake us, our Father, but lead us safely through all the changes of this present world, with an unchanging love for you, and with a holy peace of mind which comes from an assurance of your steadfast love for us, until we come at last to see you face to face, be with you where you are, behold your glory and worship you forever, through Jesus Christ, our Lord, Amen.

Short Memos to God

Lord, in my every word and action, may I become a reflection of the one who came to earth and lived a perfect life so that I might be reunited with you.

—Tracy Macon Sumner

John Jewel

Merciful Father, we plead with you, for your mercy's sake, continue your grace and favor toward us. Let not the sun of your gospel ever go down out of our hearts; let your truth abide and be established among us forever. Help our unbelief, increase our faith, and give us hearts to consider the time of our journey on earth. Through faith clothe us with Christ, that he may live in us, and your name may be glorified through us in all the world.

The *Book of Common Prayer*

Almighty God, who has given your only Son to be for us both a sacrifice for sin and also an example of godly life, give us grace that we may always most thankfully receive that his inestimable benefit, and also daily endeavor ourselves to follow the blessed steps of His most holy life; through the same Jesus Christ our Lord. Amen.

Edmund Grindal

Take from us, God, the care of worldly vanities; make us content with only the necessaries of life. Keep our hearts from delighting in honors, treasures, and pleasures of this life, and put in us a desire to be with you in your eternal kingdom. Give us Lord, such taste and feeling for your unspeakable joys in heaven that we may always long for them, and saying, with all your people, "Hasten your kingdom, Lord, take us to yourself"; for the sake of Jesus Christ, who lives and reigns, ever one God, world without end. Amen.

Short Memos to God

O most tender and gentle Lord Jesus, teach me so to contemplate you that I may become like you, and love you sincerely and simply as you have loved me.

—John Henry Newman

Thomas Cranmer

Jesus, who in almighty power was meek, and in perfect excellence was lowly, grant to us the same mind, that we may mourn over our evil will. Our bodies are frail and fading; our minds are blind and disobedient; all that we have which is our own is nothing; if we have any good in us it is wholly your gift. Savior, since you, the Lord of heaven and earth, humbled yourself, grant to us true humility, and make us like yourself; and then, of your infinite goodness, raise us to your everlasting glory; you who live and reign with the Father and the Holy Ghost forever and ever. Amen.

Short Memos to God

God, with your light and your Spirit guide our souls, our thoughts and all our actions, that we may teach your Word, that your healing power may be in us and in your church worldwide.

—Philip Melanchthon

Tracy Macon Sumner

Lord, I am selfish, but you are all about serving others in the name of your Father. I am doubtful, but you trusted your heavenly Father to the very point of dying for him. When it comes to temptation, I am weak, but you were a perfect picture of strength when the devil came to tempt you. I am prone to anger when I feel someone is misjudging me, but you were our example of "turning the other cheek." In all these things and others, Lord, make me more and more like you every day.

Catherine of Genoa

Lord, I make you a present of myself. I do not know what to do with myself. So let me make this exchange: I will place myself entirely in your hands, if you will cover my ugliness with your beauty, and tame my unruliness with your love. Put out the flames of false passion in my heart, since these flames destroy all that is true within me. Make me always busy in your service.

Lord, I want no special signs, nor am I looking for intense emotions in response to your love. I would rather be free of all emotion than to run the danger of falling victim once again to false passion. Let my love for you be naked, without any emotional clothing.

Short Memos to God

One thing we ask of you, our God, not to cease your work in our improvement. Let us look toward you, by whatever means, and be fruitful in good works.

—Ludwig van Beethoven

Thomas à Kempis

Grant me, Lord, to know what I ought to know, to love what I ought to love, to praise what delights you most, to value what is precious in your sight, to hate what is offensive to you. Do not allow me to judge according to the sight of my eyes, nor to pass sentence according to the hearing of the ears of ignorant men; but to discern with a true judgment between things visible and spiritual, and above all, always to inquire what is the good please of your will.

***

Lord Jesus, because your way is narrow and despised by the world, grant that I may despise the world and imitate you. For the servant is not greater than his Lord, nor the disciple above the Master. Let your servant be trained in your life, for there is my salvation and true holiness. Whatever else I read or hear does not fully refresh or delight me.

Henry Alford

God, who has commanded us to be perfect as you are perfect; put into my heart, I pray to you, a continual desire to obey your holy will. Teach me day by day what you would have me to do, and give me grace and power to fulfill the same. May I never, from love of ease, decline the path you point out, nor, from fear of shame, turn away from it.

Short Memos to God

Clothe me with yourself, eternal truth, so that I may live this earthly life with true obedience, and with the light of your most holy faith.

—Catherine of Siena

Celtic Prayer

This morning, as I kindle the fire upon my hearth, I pray that the flame of God's love may burn in my heart, and the hearts of all I meet today. I pray that no envy and malice, no hatred or fear, may smother the flame. I pray that indifference and apathy, contempt and pride, may not pour like cold water on the fire. Instead, may the spark of God's love light the love in my heart, that it may burn brightly through the day. And may I warm those that are lonely, whose hearts are cold and lifeless, so that all may know the comfort of God's love.

Imitating Jesus

(Based on the writings of Thomas à Kempis)

"We do this by keeping our eyes on Jesus, on whom our faith depends from start to finish." (Hebrews 12:2)

"If you follow me, you won't be stumbling through the darkness," the Lord Jesus Christ said. These words of Christ tell us that if we want to be truly enlightened and saved from all darkness of heart, we should do everything we can to imitate his life and ways.

We should make focusing and meditating on the life of Jesus a priority in our lives. When we do that, we will see that his ways and teachings exceed those of all other "holy" men.

When we have his Holy Spirit, we will then be able to discover and understand the mysterious truths of Christ. Sadly, however, too many people hear the gospel of Christ but aren't changed for the better. That's because they don't have his Spirit.

Those who come to a place of fully understanding and personally embracing the words and ways of Jesus Christ, as they are recorded in the Bible, must then endeavor to conform his or her life fully to his life. That happens as we learn his life and ways then, through the power of the Holy Spirit, make his ways our ways.

Eloquent speaking and thinking does not justify a man or woman before God, but a life like that of Christ makes him or her one of God's very own. What does it profit you if you know the whole Bible by heart and understand the teachings of all the philosophers if you didn't know the love and grace of God, as it was demonstrated in the life of Jesus Christ? Unless you make serving and loving God the way Jesus did your priority, everything else in life is vanity of vanities.

There is no higher wisdom than to disdain the thinking and ways of the world and instead tend toward the kingdom of heaven. That is exactly what Jesus did as he walked the earth as a man.

Chapter 12

Contentment and Satisfaction in God

The Bible tells us that our God meets all our needs—our physical needs and our spiritual needs alike. But there is another need our God wants to meet within us, and that's an emotional one.

God wants each and every one of us to find our inner contentment and satisfaction in him and him alone. Not in what he does for us—as worthy of praise as that is—and not for what we ask him to do for others. Not in even the very best gifts he has given us through this world and this realm of life.

During a difficult time in his life, King David wrote this prayer of contentment and satisfaction in his God:

"O God, you are my God; I earnestly search for you. My soul thirsts for you; my whole body longs for you in this parched and weary land where there is no water. I have seen you in your sanctuary and gazed upon your power and glory. Your unfailing love is better to me than life itself; how I praise you! I will honor you as long as I live, lifting up my hands to you in prayer. You satisfy me more than the richest of foods. I will praise you with songs of joy." (Psalm 63:1–5)

David's life, as great and blessed as it was, wasn't always easy. He went through times where he had to hide out in the desert to avoid capture and murder at the hands of his enemies. But David kept his eyes on the fact that his God was everything to him.

This chapter is made up of the prayers of men and women of God who had already either made him their source of contentment or who recognized their need to put him in that place in their hearts and lives.

Basil the Great

Lord our God, teach us, we pray, to ask you in the right way for the right blessings. Steer the ship of our lives towards yourself, the tranquil haven of all storm-tossed souls. Show us the course in which we should go. Renew a willing spirit within us. Let your Spirit curb our wayward senses, and guide and enable us toward that which is our true good to keep your laws, and in all we do to rejoice always in your glorious and gladdening presence. For yours is the glory and praise from all your saints forever and ever.

Gregory of Nazianzus

Lord, as I read the psalms let me hear you singing. As I read your words, let me hear you speaking. As I reflect on each page, let me see your image. And as I seek to put your precepts into practice, let my heart be filled with joy.

John Knox

Let your mighty outstretched arm, Lord God, be our defense; your mercy and loving-kindness in Jesus Christ, your dear Son, our salvation; your true word our instruction; the grace of your life-giving Spirit our comfort and consolation, to the end and in the end; through the same Jesus Christ our Lord.

Christina Rossetti

Lord seek us, Lord find us
In your patient care,
Be your love before us, behind us,

Lest he bait a snare,
Lest he forge a chain to bind us,
Lest he speak us fair,
Turn not from us, call to mind us,
Find, embrace us, hear.
Be your love before us, behind us,
Round us everywhere.

John Newton

May the grace of Christ our Savior,
And the Father's boundless love,
With the Holy Spirit's favor,
Rest upon us from above.

Thus may we abide in union
With each other and the Lord,
And possess, in sweet communion,
Joys which earth cannot afford.

Ambrose of Milan

Lord, teach me to seek you, and reveal yourself to me when I seek you.
For I cannot seek you unless you first teach me, nor find you unless you
first reveal yourself to me. Let me seek you in longing and long for you
in seeking. Let me find you in love and love you in finding.

Richard Baxter

Keep me, Lord, while I wait here on this earth, in a serious seeking
after you, and in an affectionate walking with you, every day of my life
so that when you come, I may be found not hiding my talent, nor serving the flesh, nor yet asleep with my lamp unfurnished, but waiting and
longing for you.

Thomas à Kempis

Ah, Lord God, you holy lover of my soul, when you come into my soul,
all that is within me shall rejoice. You are my glory and the delight of
my heart. You are my hope and refuge in the day of my trouble. Set me

free from all evil passions, and heal my heart of all undue affections; that, being inwardly cured and thoroughly cleansed, I may be made fit to love, courageous to suffer, steady to persevere. Nothing is sweeter than Love, nothing more courageous, nothing fuller nor better in heaven and earth; because love is born of God, and cannot rest but in God, above all created things. Let me love you more than myself, nor love myself but for you. Amen.

 **Short Memos to God**

Lord, you are my lover, my longing, my flowing stream, my sun, and I am your reflection.

—Mechthild of Magdeburg

Celtic Prayer

My soul's desire is to see the face of God, and to rest in his house.

My soul's desire is to study the Scriptures, and to learn the ways of God.

My soul's desire is to be freed from all fear and sadness, and to share Christ's risen life.

My soul's desire is to imitate my King, and to sing his praises always.

My soul's desire is to enter the gates of heaven, and to gaze upon the light that shines forever.

Dear Lord, you alone know what my soul truly desires; and you alone can satisfy those desires.

Tracy Macon Sumner

Lord, may there never be a moment of any day when I am not aware of your presence within me. You have created me to have perfect fellowship with yourself, and you have given me Jesus Christ so that we could enjoy that fellowship unbroken. Let me always remember that there is nothing that can take your place in this life or the life to come.

John Oxenham

Through every minute of this day, be with me, Lord!
Through every day of all this week, be with me, Lord!
Through every week of all this year, be with me, Lord!
So shall the days and weeks and years be threaded on a golden cord.
And all draw on with sweet accord into thy fullness, Lord, that so,
When time is past,
By grace I may, at last,
Be with thee, Lord.

Short Memos to God

My God, I pray that I may so know you and love you
that I may rejoice in you. Let me receive that which you
promised through your truth that my joy may be full.

—Anselm of Canterbury

Irenaeus of Lyons

Christ Jesus, when all is darkness and we feel our weakness and
helplessness, give us the sense of your presence, your love, and your
strength. Help us to have perfect trust in your protecting love and
strengthening power, so that nothing may frighten or worry us, for,
living close to you, we shall see your hand, your purpose, and your will
through all things.

Ignatius of Loyola

I appeal to you, Lord, God of Abraham, God of Isaac, God of Jacob
and Israel, you the Father of our Lord Jesus Christ. Infinitely merciful
as you are, it is your will that we should learn to know you. You made
heaven and earth, you rule supreme over all that is. You are the true,
the only God; there is no other god above you. Through our Lord
Jesus Christ and the gifts of the Holy Spirit, grant that all who read
what I have written here may know you, because you alone are God;
let them draw strength from you; keep them from all teaching that is
heretical, irreligious or godless.

Ambrose of Milan

Lord, you have mercy on all. Take away from me my sins, and mercifully set me ablaze with the fire of your Holy Spirit. Take away from me the heart of stone, and give me a human heart, a heart to love and adore you, a heart to delight in you, to follow and enjoy you, for Christ's sake.

 **Short Memos to God**

God, be all to me: all my love, hope, and striving. Let my thoughts and words flow from you, my everyday life be in you, and every breath I take be for you.

—John Cassian

John Scotus Erigena

Everlasting essence of things beyond space and time, and yet within them: you transcend yet pervade all things. Manifest yourself to us who feel after you, seeking you in the shadows of our ignorance. Stretch forth your hand to help us, for we can't come to you without your aid. Reveal yourself to us, for we seek nothing but you.

Guigo the Carthusian

Lord, you are invisible, except to the pure of heart. I seek to understand true purity of heart by reading the Scriptures and meditating. Lord, I have read your words and meditated on your person for more years than I can remember. I long to see you face to face. It is the sight of you Lord, that I have sought. Over the years, the fire of desire to see you has grown hotter and hotter. As I have meditated, my soul has received greater light. And the scriptures excite my soul more than ever. Lord, I do not dare to call you to reveal yourself now or soon. Give me a sign, a promise, to ensure me that one day I will be rewarded. Give me a single drop of heavenly rain to quench my spiritual thirst.

John Cosin

Lord, be a light to my eyes, music to my ears, sweetness to my taste, and a full contentment to my heart. Be my sunshine in the day, my food at the table, my rest in the night, my clothing in nakedness, and my provider in all necessities. Lord, Jesus, I give you my body, my soul, my substance, my fame, my friends, my liberty, and my life. Dispose of me and all that is mine, as it seems best to you and to the glory of your blessed name.

James S. Bell Jr.

Dear Lord, you have said in your Holy Word that godliness with contentment is great gain. Keep us from a materialistic spirit that constantly seeks for more earthly possessions. Help us remember that we are to seek first the Kingdom of God and the things we really need will be added. Let us store our treasures in heaven and "travel light" while here on earth. Let us, however, never be content with our spiritual condition but strive with our whole hearts to improve and grow more like you.

Jeremy Taylor

Lord Jesus, come quickly. My heart desires your presence, and would entertain you, not as a guest but as an inhabitant, as the Lord of all my faculties. Enter in and take possession, and dwell with me forever, that I may also dwell in the heart of my dearest Lord, which was opened for me with a spear and love.

Short Memos to God

I beg you, most loving Savior, to reveal yourself to me, that knowing you I may desire you, that desiring you I may love you, that loving you I may always hold you in my thoughts.

—Columbanus

Brooke Foss Westcott

Lord God, in whom we live and move and have our being, open our eyes that we may see your fatherly presence ever about us. Draw our hearts to you with the power of love. Teach us in nothing to be anxious; and when we have done what you have given us to do, help us, our God and Savior, to leave the issue to your wisdom. Take from us all doubt and distrust. Lift our thoughts up to yourself, and make us know that all things are possible to us, and through your Son our redeemer, Jesus Christ our Lord.

Teresa of Avila

If the love you bear me, Lord, is like mine for you, tell me, why do I hesitate? And why do you delay? *What do you want from me, O soul?* "Only to see you, my God" *And what do you fear the most?* "My greatest fear is losing you." When a soul is gathered to God what more could it desire than to love and love still more, and being immersed in that love to love again? I ask you, Lord, for such a complete love that the soul may possess you and may make itself a home in the place that is most fitting.

Augustine of Hippo

My God, let me know and love you, so that I may find my happiness in you. Since I cannot fully achieve this on earth, help me to improve daily until I may do so to the full. Enable me to know you ever more on earth, so that I may know you perfectly in heaven. Enable me to love you ever more on earth, so that I may love you perfectly in heaven. In that way my joy may be great on earth, and perfect with you in heaven.

God of truth, grant me the happiness of heaven so that my joy may be full in accord with your promise. In the meantime, let my mind dwell on that happiness, my tongue speak of it, my heart pine for it, my mouth pronounce it, my soul hunger for it, my flesh thirst for it, and my entire being desire it until I enter through death in the joy of my Lord forever. Amen.

Short Memos to God

Let my eyes penetrate the veil, and tear off the mask, that I can see your truth face to face.

—John of the Cross

Claude de la Colombiere

My God, I believe most firmly that you watch over all who hope in you, and that we will need nothing when we rely upon you in all things. Therefore I am resolved for the future to cast all my cares upon you.

People may deprive me of worldly goods and status. Sickness may take from me my strength and the means of serving you. I may even jeopardize our relationship by sin, but my trust shall never leave me. I will preserve it to the last moment of my life, and the powers of hell shall seek in vain to grab it from me.

Let others seek happiness in their wealth and in their talents. Let them trust in the purity of their lives, the severity of their mortifications, in the number of their good works, the enthusiasm of their prayers, as for me, my rock and my refuge, my confidence in you fills me with hope. For you, my divine protector, alone have settled me in hope.

Our Father ...

(Adapted from the writings of Francis of Assisi and inspired by the Lord's Prayer)

Our Father: Our Creator, Redeemer, Comforter, and Savior.

In heaven: You are with the angels and the saints, bathing them in your light that they may be enlightened by your love, and dwelling within them that they may be filled with your joy. You are the supreme good, the eternal good, from whom comes all goodness, and without whom there is no goodness.

May your name be honored: May our knowledge of you become ever clearer, that we may know the breadth of your blessings, the length of your promises, the height of your majesty, and the depth of your judgments.

May your kingdom come soon: Rule in our hearts with your grace, that we may become fit subjects for your kingdom. We desire nothing more than to dwell in your kingdom, where we can watch you on your throne, and enjoy your perfect love.

Your will be done here on earth just as it is in heaven: May we love you with our whole heart by always thinking of you, with our whole soul by always desiring you, with our whole mind by directing all our intentions to you, and with our whole strength by spending all our energies in your service. And may we love our neighbors as ourselves, drawing them to your love, rejoicing in their good fortunes, and caring for them in their misfortunes.

Give us our food today: In memory and understanding and reverence of the love which our Lord Jesus Christ has for us, revealed by his sacrifice for us on the cross, we ask for the perfect bread of his body.

And forgive us our sins today: We know that you forgive us, through the suffering and death of your beloved Son.

Just as we have forgiven those who have sinned against us: Enable us to forgive perfectly and without reserve any wrong that has been committed against us. And strengthen our hearts truly to love our enemies, praying for them and striving to serve them.

And don't let us yield to temptation: Save us not only from obvious and persistent temptations, but also those that are hidden or come suddenly when our guard is lowered.

But deliver us from the evil one: Protect us from past evil, protect us against present evil, and free us from future evil.

Gilbert of Hoyland

When, good Lord, will you manifest yourself to us in bright sunshine? Yes, we are slow to understand and slow to see. But we are quick to believe that if you chose to reveal yourself to us, you could do so this very day. Dear Lord, please appear to us, at dawn or at dusk or at the height of the day. Come to our table at mealtimes, that we may share our meals with you. Come to our bed, that we may share our rest with you. Come to our prayers so that we may rejoice and be glad.

Benedict of Nursia

Gracious and holy Father, give us wisdom to perceive you, intelligence to understand you, diligence to seek you, patience to wait for you, eyes to behold you, a heart to meditate on you, and a life to proclaim you; through the power of the Spirit of Jesus Christ our Lord.

Short Memos to God

May the love of the Word made flesh enfold us, his joy fill our lives, his peace be in our hearts; and the blessing of God be with us this night and always.

—*Celebrating Common Prayer*

Symeon the New Theologian

Come, true light.
Come, eternal life.
Come, hidden mystery.
Come, indescribable treasure.
Come, ineffable thing.
Come, inconceivable person.
Come, endless delight.
Come, unsetting light.
Come, true and fervent expectation of all those who will be saved.
Come, rising of those who lie down.
Come, resurrection of the dead.
Come, powerful one, who always creates and re-creates and transforms by your will alone.
Come, invisible and totally intangible and untouchable.
Come, you who always remain immobile and at each moment move all, and come to us, who lie in Hades, you who are above all heavens.
Come, desirable and legendary name, which is completely impossible for us to express what you are or to know your nature.

Come, eternal joy.

Come, unwithering wreath.

Come, purple of the great king our God.

Come, crystalline cincture, studded with precious stones.

Come, inaccessible sandal.

Come, royal robe and truly imperial right hand.

Come, you whom my wretched soul has desired and does desire.

Come, you who alone go to the lonely for as you see I am lonely.

Come, you who have separated me from everything and made me solitary in this world.

Come, you who have become yourself desire in me, who have made me desire you, the absolutely inaccessible one.

Come, my breath and life.

Come, consolation of my humble soul.

Come, my joy, my glory, and my endless delight.

Robert Leighton

Grant, Lord, that I may be so ravished in the wonder of your love that I may forget myself and all things, that I may feel neither prosperity nor adversity, that I may not fear to suffer all the pain in the world rather than be parted from you. Let me find you more inwardly and verily present with me than I am with myself. And make me the most circumspect how I do use myself in your presence, my holy Lord.

Short Memos to God

Teach us, God, not to torture ourselves, not to make martyrs of ourselves through stifling reflection. Teach us rather to breathe deeply in faith, through Jesus, our Lord.

—Søren Kierkegaard

Gerard W. Hughes

Lord, deliver us from searching for our ultimate security in any created thing, in any theory, system or organization, sacred or secular. Show yourself to us, our light, our refuge, our salvation, so that we may recognize you in all things and worship you always in spirit and in truth.

Augustine of Hippo

Lord Jesus, let me know myself and know you and desire nothing but you. Let me hate myself and love you. Let me do everything for your sake. Let me humble myself and acclaim you. Let me think nothing except you. Let me die to myself and live in you. Let me accept whatever happens as coming from you. Let me banish self and follow you and always desire to follow you. Let me fly from myself and take refuge in you so that I may deserve to be defended by you. Let me fear for myself, let me fear you, and let me be among those you have chosen. Let me distrust myself and put my trust in you. Let me be willing to obey for your sake. Let me cling to nothing but you, and let me be poor because of you. Look upon me, that I may love you. Call me that I may see you and forever enjoy you.

Joy in the Lord's Sufficiency

(Adapted from the writings of James Hudson Taylor)

"Don't be dejected and sad, for the joy of the LORD is your strength." (Nehemiah 8:10)

What is "the joy of the Lord" that he calls our strength? Is it joy that there is such a Lord? For we cannot realize that He exists without joy. Or is it joy that *He* is our Lord? For possession of Him is a fruitful source of joy. Or, again, is it joy that He has imparted to us and shed abroad in our hearts by His Spirit? Or, lastly, is it *His own joy* that is our strength? While all these sources of joy are ours, there is no doubt that it is the last of them to which this verse specifically refers.

John 15:11 refers to our Savior's joy in the bearing of fruit through His branches. It was His will that His joy might remain in them and that, consequently, their joy might be full. Here we see the joy of the Lord distinguished from the joy of His people.

In Hebrews 12:2, we have the joy of the Lord in the redemption of His people—joy to despise the shame and endure the cross. It was strength for self-sacrifice.

In Zephaniah 3:17, we have the joy of the Lord in the possession of His purchased inheritance. How wonderful is this joy! "He will rejoice over you with great gladness. With his love, he will calm all your fears. He will exult over you by singing a happy song."

It is the consciousness of the threefold joy of the Lord—His joy in ransoming us, His joy in dwelling within us as our Savior and power for bearing fruit, and His joy in possessing us as His bride and His delight—that is our real strength. Our joy in Him may fluctuate, but His joy in us knows no change.

Chapter 13

Prayers of Compassion and Service to Others

During his earthly ministry, Jesus taught his disciples the importance of expressing through word and deed godly compassion for their fellow man as they preached the gospel.

Jesus said: "For I was hungry, and you fed me. I was thirsty, and you gave me a drink. I was a stranger, and you invited me into your home. I was naked, and you gave me clothing. I was sick, and you cared for me. I was in prison, and you visited me. ... I assure you, when you did it to one of the least of these my brothers and sisters, you were doing it to me!" (Matthew 25:25–36, 40)

Throughout the history of Christianity, many believers have taken those words very seriously and have expressed their devotion to Christ by feeding the hungry, giving water to the thirsty, clothing the naked, caring for the sick, and visiting those in prison.

Likewise, Christian history has left us with literally hundreds of prayers of compassion for our fellow human beings, some of which have become traditions of the Roman Catholics and Protestants alike. In this chapter, we look at some examples.

Alan Stewart Paton

Lord, open my eyes that I may see the needs of others, open my ears that I may hear their cries, open my heart so that they need not be without relief. Let me not be afraid to defend the weak because of the anger of the strong, nor afraid to defend the poor because of the anger of the rich. Show me where love and hope and faith are needed, and use me to bring them to these places. Open my eyes and ears that I may, this coming day, be able to do some work of peace for you.

Short Memos to God

Use me then, my Savior, for whatever purpose and in whatever way you may require. Here is my poor heart, an empty vessel; fill it with your grace.

—D. L. Moody

Mother Teresa of Calcutta

Lord by your grace, let the poor see me be drawn to Christ and invite him to enter their homes and their lives. Let the sick and the suffering find in me a real angel of comfort and consolation. Let the little ones of the streets cling to me because I remind them of him, the friend of all little ones.

***

Dear Jesus, help me to spread your fragrance everywhere I go. Flood my soul with your spirit and life. Penetrate and possess my whole being so utterly that my life may only be a radiance of yours. Shine through me and be so in me that every soul I come in contact with may feel your presence in my soul. Let them look up and see no longer me but only Jesus! Stay with me and then I shall begin to shine as you shine, so to shine as you to be a light to others; the light, O Jesus, will be all from you; none of it will be mine: it will be you shining on others through me. Let me thus praise you in the way you love best: by shining on those around me. Let me preach you without preaching, not by words, but by my example, by the catching force, the sympathetic influence of what I do, the evident fullness of the love my heart bears to you.

***

Dearest Lord, may I see you today and every day in the person of your sick, and, while nursing them, minister unto you. Though you hide yourself behind the unattractive disguise of the irritable, the exacting, the unreasonable, may I still recognize you, and say, "Jesus, my patient Lord, how sweet it is to serve you.

Peter Marshall

Lord Jesus, bless all who serve us, who have dedicated their lives to the ministry of others—all the teachers of our schools who labor so patiently with so little appreciation; all who wait upon the public, the clerks in the stores who have to accept criticism, complaints, bad manners, and selfishness at the hands of a thoughtless public. Bless the mailman, the drivers of streetcars and buses who must listen to people who lose their tempers. Bless every humble soul who, in these days of stress and strain, preaches sermons without words. Amen.

Short Memos to God

Make us worthy Lord, to serve our fellow men throughout the world who live and die in poverty and hunger. Give them, through our hands, this day their daily bread, and by our understanding love, give peace and joy.
—Mother Teresa of Calcutta

A Prayer of Christian Aid

Lord, change our Christianity from words into action. Turn our good intentions into commitment. Transform our trackless wandering into a pilgrimage. Lead us out to our brothers and sisters overseas, that we may catch their sense of urgency, share their courage against sin and corruption, their strength against oppression.

Lord, we are taught that our way is the only way of justice, peace, and love. If we are facing in the wrong direction, turn us around.

Reinhold Niebuhr

Our God who has bound us together in this bundle of life, give us grace to understand how our lives depend upon the courage, the industry, the honesty and the integrity of our fellow men so that we may be mindful of their needs, grateful for their faithfulness, and faithful to our responsibilities to them.

Inazo Nitobe

I ask, Lord, for daily bread, but not for wealth, lest I forget the poor. I ask for strength, but not for power, lest I despise the meek. I ask for wisdom, but not for learning, lest I condemn the simple. I ask for a clean name, but not for fame, lest I condemn the lowly. I ask for peace of mind, but not for idle hours, lest I fail to hearken to the call of duty.

Rabindranath Tagore

Hands who touched the leper, touch my wounded heart;
Hands who healed the blind man, heal my aching soul;
Hands who cured the lame, mend my disjointed life;
Hands who embraced all life, enfold me in your peace.
Lord, merely touch and heal, cure and forgive

This is my prayer to you, my Lord;
Give me strength lightly to bear my joys and sorrows;
Give me the strength to make my love fruitful in service;
Give me the strength never to disown the poor or bend my knees before insolent might.
Give me the strength to raise my mind high above daily trifles.
And give me the strength to surrender my strength to thy will with love.

Tracy Macon Sumner

Lord, you were a perfect example of serving your Father through service to humankind. I ask you to lead me and direct me to those who need a demonstration of God's love through an act of service. I know that there are opportunities to serve in my own neighborhood, and I ask you to do what you must to bring them to my attention.

Brooke Foss Westcott

Our heavenly Father, by whose providence the duties of men are variously ordered, grant to us all such a spirit that we may labor heartily to do our work in our several stations, as serving one Master and looking for one reward. Teach us to put to good use whatever talents you have given us, and enable us to redeem our time by patience and zeal.

Frederick D. Maurice

Eternal Father, we believe that in your Son you are satisfied with our race. We believe that you have created us in him, and that you look upon us as we really are, not as we are made by the unbelief which separates us from you and from our brethren. Only thus, do we find that peace your Son left his disciples. We believe that in Christ you will restore all things. Use us, each one of us, we humbly ask you, to work with you in your purpose of restoration, blotting out our sins, that we may serve you day by day with free hearts.

Short Memos to God

Strengthen us, our God, to relieve the oppressed, to hear the groans of poor prisoners, to reform the abuses from all professionals, that many be made not poor to make a few rich.

—Oliver Cromwell

A Celtic Prayer

Let us go forth
In the goodness of our merciful Father,
In the gentleness of our brother Jesus,
In the radiance of his Holy Spirit,
In the faith of the apostles,
In the joyful praise of the angels,
In the holiness of the saints,
In the courage of the martyrs.

Let us go forth
In the wisdom of our all-seeing Father,
In the patience of our all-loving brother,
In the learning of the apostles,
In the gracious guidance of the angels,
In the patience of the saints,
In the self-control of the martyrs.

Such is the path for all servants of Christ,
The path from death to eternal life.

 **Short Memos to God**

Lord, give us such a strong love for you as may sweeten
our obedience. Let us not serve you with the spirit of
bondage as slaves, but with cheerfulness and gladness,
rejoicing in your work.

—Benjamin Jenks

William Temple

God of love, we pray that you give us love: love in our thinking, love
in our speaking, love in our doing, and love in the hidden places of our
souls; love of our neighbors, near and far; love of our friends, old and
new; love of those whom we find it hard to bear, and love of those we
find it hard to bear with us; love of those with whom we work, and love
of those with whom we take our ease; love in joy, love in sorrow; love in
life and love in death; that so at length we may be worthy to dwell with
you, who are eternal Love, Father, Son, and Holy Spirit, forever and
ever.

Edward Lambe Parsons

Heavenly Father, whose blessed Son came not to be served but to serve:
bless all who, following in his steps, give themselves to the service of
others; that with wisdom, patience and courage, they may minister in
his name to the suffering, the friendless and the needy. This for the
love of him who laid down his life for us, your Son our Savior Jesus
Christ, who lives and reigns with you and the Holy Spirit, one God forever and ever.

Doing as Jesus Did, Not Just as He Said

(Adapted from the writings of Matthew Henry)

"Whoever wants to be a leader among you must be your servant, and whoever wants to be first must become your slave. For even I, the Son of Man, came here not to be served but to serve others, and to give my life as a ransom for many." (Matthew 20:26–28)

How are the servants of Jesus Christ to be different from the rest of the world? Before, Jesus had implied it, but now he says it: "Whoever wants to be a leader among you must be your servant, and whoever wants to be first must become your slave."

Jesus wanted his disciples to understand that it was their duty to humbly and effectively build one another up through serving. That means being ready and willing to stoop down and do the lowliest duties, and it means doing that out of love for one another. It means that each disciple of Christ must be willing to submit to others and to regard others as better than himself or herself.

The New Testament tells us that we should submit to one another (1 Peter 5:5, Ephesians 5:21), build one another up (Romans 14:19), and please one another so that they can be built up in their faith. (Romans 15:2) The Apostle Paul himself stated that he had made himself everyone's servant. (1 Corinthians 9:19)

It is a privilege for Jesus' followers to faithfully do the duty of serving others. When they do that, they must do so just as Jesus himself did: "For even I, the Son of Man, came here not to be served but to serve others, and to give my life as a ransom for many." (verse 28)

For the Christian, the way to be considered "great" and a leader is to serve humbly. Those who do that are to be the most highly thought of and respected in the church. These are the ones who honor God most, and they are the ones God Himself will honor.

D. L. Moody

Our Heavenly Father, we pray that you will give us more and more of the compassion of Christ. We read from the very beginning that he was moved with compassion, just like the Good Samaritan when he met this poor, wounded and dying man. God, give us the spirit of the Good Samaritan! May we go from this building and find many people and tell them of Christ and heaven. May we go to the homes of the poor drunkards. May we go to the homes and hearts of gamblers, the homes of the fallen, the despised and the outcast, and tell them of Christ and heaven. Spirit of God, come down upon this assembly, and may the church of God find out who their neighbors are.

Short Memos to God

Thank you, Lord, for giving me the opportunity to serve you through serving others. Through the blessing of your Holy Spirit, make me both equal to the task and worthy of it.

—Tracy Macon Sumner

Eugène Bersier

Our God, from whom we have received life and all earthly blessings, grant to us each day what we need. Give to us the strength to perform faithfully our appointed tasks. Bless the work of our hands and of our minds. Grant that we may always serve you, in sickness and in health, in necessity and in abundance. Bless our joys and our trials, and give us grace to seek your kingdom and its righteousness first, and give us the sure and certain faith that everything else will be added for us through Jesus Christ, your Son, our Lord and Savior.

James S. Bell Jr.

Lord I thank you that you know all about us; you know our imperfect deeds done on your behalf, our attempts to please you and our lack of perseverance as well as impure motives. Overlook our failures and take into account the love in our hearts. Thank you that it is you who creates a desire in us by your Holy Spirit, and it is you who gives us strength, power, and passion to fulfill all the good works you have ordained for us since the beginning of time. We give you the glory and credit for any success or blessing we have received as a result of our efforts on your behalf. Jesus, increase in us a desire to live as you lived for you said you did not come to be served, but to serve. You also said the servant is not greater than his master. So dear master, help us to serve in a way that shows forth your person to all we encounter.

John of Kronstadt

Lord, teach me to demonstrate charity willingly, kindly, joyfully, and help me to believe that by demonstrating it I do not lose but gain infinitely more than what I give. Turn my eyes away from hard-hearted people who do not sympathize with the poor, who meet poverty with indifference, who judge, reproach, brand it with shameful names, and weaken my heart, so that I may not do good, so that I, too, may harden my heart against poverty. My Lord, how many such people we meet! Lord, grant that every charity I take part in may be profitable and may not do harm.

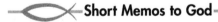

Short Memos to God

Lord, teach me to say "yes" when you bring into my life those who need to see your love put on display through simple acts of charity.

—Tracy Macon Sumner

Florence Nightingale

Oh God, you put into my heart this great desire to devote myself to the sick and sorrowful; I offer it to you. Do with it what is for your service.

Oh my Creator, are you leading every man of us to perfection? Or is this only a metaphysical idea for which there is no evidence? Is man only a constant repetition of himself? You know that through all these twenty horrible years I have been supported by the belief (I think I must believe it still or I am sure I could not work) that I was working with you who were bringing every one of us, even our poor nurses, to perfection. O Lord, even now I am trying to snatch the management of your world from your hands. Too little have I looked for something higher and better than my own world—the work of supreme Wisdom, which uses us whether we know it or not.

Robert Millman

Great Lord of the harvest, send forth, we ask you, laborers into the harvest of the world, that the grain which is even now ripe may not fall and perish through our neglect. Pour forth your sanctifying Spirit on our fellow Christians abroad, and your converting grace on those who are living in darkness. Raise up, we beg you, a devout ministry among the native believers, that, all your people being knit together in one body, in love, your church may grow up into the measure of the stature of the fullness of Christ; through him who died and rose again for us all, the same Jesus Christ our Lord.

Short Memos to God

Teach us, Lord, to give, and not to count the cost; to fight, and not to heed the wounds; to toil, and not to seek for rest; to labor, and not to ask for any reward, except knowing that we do your holy will.

—Ignatius of Loyola

Henry Alford

Lord, give us more charity, more self-denial, more likeness to you. Teach us to sacrifice our comforts to others, and our likings for the sake of doing good. Make us kindly in thought, gentle in word, generous in deed. Teach us that it is better to give than to receive, better to forget ourselves than to put ourselves forward, better to minister than to be ministered to. And to you, the God of Love, be all glory and praise, both now and forevermore.

Anthony Ashley Cooper

Our God, the Father of the forsaken, the helper of the weak, the supplier of the needy: you have poured out and proportioned your gifts to us in such a way that everyone may acknowledge and perform the joyous duty of serving one another. You teach us that love toward the human race is the bond of perfection and the initiation of your blessed self. Open our eyes and touch our hearts so that we may see and do, both for this world and for the one to come, the things that give us peace. Strengthen me in the work I have undertaken. Give me counsel and wisdom, perseverance, faith and zeal. And in your own good time, and according to your will, prosper my work. Pour into me a spirit of humility. Let me do nothing outside of a commitment to obedience to your will, thankfulness for your unspeakable mercies, and love for your adorable Son, Christ Jesus.

Short Memos to God

Lord, baptize our hearts into a sense of the needs and conditions of all.

—George Fox

Theresa of Avila

How is it, my God, that you have given me this hectic busy life when I have so little time to enjoy your presence. Throughout the day people are waiting to speak with me, and even at meals I have to continue talking to people about their needs and problems. During sleep itself, I am still thinking and dreaming about the multitude of concerns that surround me. I do all this not for my own sake but for yours. To me my present pattern of life is a torment; I only hope that for you it is a sacrifice of love. I know that you are constantly beside me, yet I am usually so busy that I ignore you. If you want me to remain so busy, please force me to think about and love you even in the midst of such hectic activity. If you do not want me so busy, please release me from it, showing how others can take over my responsibility.

***

God of love, help us to remember that Christ has no body now on earth but ours, no hands but ours, no feet but ours. Ours are the eyes that see the needs of the world. Ours are the hands with which to bless everyone now. Ours are the feet with which he is to go about doing good.

Francis Xavier

O God of all the nations of the earth, remember the many people who, though they are created in your image, have not known you or the dying of your Son, their Savior Jesus Christ. Grant that by the prayers and labors of your holy church they may be delivered from all ignorance and unbelief and brought to worship you.

Short Memos to God

Thank you, Lord Jesus, that you will be our hiding place, whatever happens. Lord Jesus, you suffered for me—what am I suffering for you?

—Corrie ten Boom

Martin Luther

Lord God, you have appointed me as a pastor in your church, but you see how unsuited I am to meet so great and difficult a task. If I had lacked your help, I would have ruined everything long ago. Therefore, I call on you. I wish to devote my mouth and my heart to you. I shall teach the people. I myself will learn and ponder diligently upon your Word. Use me as your instrument—but do not leave me, for if I were ever on my own, I would easily wreck it all.

Prayer of Service (Author Unknown)

May I become at all times, both now and forever
A protector for those without protection
A guide for those who have lost their way
A ship for those with oceans to cross
A bridge for those with rivers to cross
A sanctuary for those in danger
A lamp for those without light
A place of refuge for those who lack shelter
And a servant to all in need.

Francis of Assisi (the Prayer of St. Francis)

Lord, make me an instrument of your peace.
Where there is hatred, let me sow love,
Where there is offence, pardon,
Where there is discord, unity,
Where there is doubt, faith,
Where there is error, truth,
Where there is despair, hope,
Where there is sadness, joy,
Where there is darkness, light.

O Divine Master, grant that I may not so much seek
To be consoled as to console,
To be understood as to understand,
To be loved as to love.
For it is in giving that we receive,
It is in pardoning that we are pardoned,
It is in dying that we are born to eternal life.

Short Memos to God

Grant, Lord, that the course of this world may be so peaceably be ordered by your governance that your church may joyfully serve you in all godly quietness.

—The *Leonine Sacramentary*

Request for People to Serve (Author Unknown)

Lord, when I am hungry, give me someone to feed. When I am thirsty, give me water for their thirst. When I am sad, give me someone to lift from sorrow. When burdens weigh upon me, lay upon my shoulders the burden of my fellows. When I stand greatly in need of tenderness, give me someone who yearns for love. May your will be my bread, your grace my strength, your love my resting place.

Augustine of Hippo

Lord, who though you were rich yet for our sakes became poor, and has promised in your holy gospel that whatever is done for the least of your brethren you will receive as done to you: give us grace, we humbly ask you, to be always willing and ready to minister, as you enable us, to the needs of others, and to extend the blessings of your kingdom over all the world.

The Seriousness of Serving God

(Adapted from the writings of George Campbell Morgan)

"Aaron's sons Nadab and Abihu put coals of fire in their incense burners and sprinkled incense over it. In this way, they disobeyed the Lord by burning before him a different kind of fire than he had commanded." (Leviticus 10:1)

There is no question that this is a story we should take very seriously as it causes those who are called to service to stop and think. It also reminds us that it is necessary to be constantly and continually loyal to God when it comes to our methods of serving Him. It challenges the Christian church to stop now and again to reexamine and readjust its relationship with the Lord. It also calls us to scrutinize every service organization that springs up to see that they are working in harmony with God's methods.

It is possible that if the church would give itself this kind of examination and readjustment that it would find that many of these organizations are merely hangers-on that sap the life of the church and contribute nothing to the work of God.

When we step away from the bigger picture and look at some particulars, we see that this verse gives us a very solemn message concerning our work for God. The dark and ominous hint in this story is one we need to emphasize in its application to us: those who work for God must never approach His work with wrong motivations. To attempt God's work out of a desire for fame or notoriety is to put on His altar false burnt offerings.

We are no longer bound to prescribed forms of service. The Spirit of the living and ever-present God is with us now, and our most important priority when it comes to our Christian service is that we seek to know God's will and submit ourselves to His direction.

Part 4

Prayers for Special Occasions

There are seasons in life when even what might otherwise be
a powerful, life-altering prayer just won't do. These are special occasions that need special prayer. The next four chapters
examine how to pray during those special times: times such as
the holidays, specific life seasons (baptism, death, marriage), and
parenthood. These kinds of prayers make the most memorable—
and trying—life event an avenue for the special blessings of God.

Chapter 14

Prayers for the "Holy" Days

Of all the memorable things Jesus did and said during his earthly ministry, three events during his time on Earth stand out, even for many who don't actively practice Christianity: his birth, his death, and his resurrection from the dead.

People throughout the world celebrate Christmas, which, in the religious sense, commemorates the birth of Jesus Christ. Many others recognize Good Friday, which marks the day that Jesus was crucified. And still others celebrate Easter, which is the observance of the resurrection.

Christian tradition is chock-full of prayers and poems to God celebrating these three events—some that come directly from the Bible and some that were written and spoken by Christian leaders during the twenty-century history of Christianity.

'Tis the Season

In the cultures that celebrate Christmas, it has come to be known as a season of celebration and giving. But the prayers and writings of many believers throughout Christian history recognize what Christmas really means: the birth of Jesus.

Mary's Song of Praise

One of the best-known and most-loved prayers in all of the Bible is found in the second chapter of the gospel of Luke. (Luke 1:46–55) It is a song of praise by the Virgin Mary, the mother of Jesus Christ. It has come to be known as the "Magnificat," and it reads like this:

Oh, how I praise the Lord.
How I rejoice in God my Savior!
For he took notice of his lowly servant girl,
and now generation after generation will call me blessed.
For he, the Mighty One, is holy
and he has done great things for me.
His mercy goes on from generation to generation
to all who fear him.
His mighty arm does tremendous things!
How he scatters the proud and haughty ones!
He has taken princes from their thrones
and exalted the lowly.
He has satisfied the hungry with good things
and sent the rich away with empty hands.
And how he has helped his servant Israel!
He has not forgotten his promise to be merciful.
For he promised our ancestors—Abraham and his children—
to be merciful to them forever.

Short Memos to God

Good Jesus, born at this time, a little child of love for us: be born in me so that I may be a little child in love with you.
—Edward Bouverie Pusey

"The World's Desire," by Gilbert Keith Chesterton

The Christ-child lay on Mary's lap,
His hair was like a light.
(Oh weary, weary was the world,
But here is all alright.)

Ah, dearest Jesus, Holy Child,
Make your bed, soft, undefiled
Within my heart, that it may be
A quiet chamber, kept for You.
My heart for very joy does leap
My lips no more can silence keep,
I must sing with joyful tongue
That sweetest ancient cradle song.

Christ Is Born!

(John Banister Tabb, from *A Diary of Readings,* by John Baillie)

A little boy of heavenly birth,
But far from home today,
Comes down to find His ball, the earth,
That sin has cast away.

O comrades, let us one and all
Join in to get Him back His ball!

***

The Father speaking to the Son,
In all the multitude was none
That caught the meaning true.
And yet 'This word from heaven', said He,
'Was spoken not because of Me—
But came because of you.'

Thus through the Son of Man alone
The mysteries of God are known;
Thus to the chosen few.
With eye and ear attentive found

He speaks in every sense and sound,
The old beginning new.

***

Let my heart the cradle be
Of Thy bleak Nativity!
Tossed by wintry tempests wild,
If it rock Thee, Holy Child,
Then as grows the outer din,
Greater peace will reign within.

Robert Louis Stevenson

Loving Father, help us remember the birth of Jesus, that we may share in the song of the angels, the gladness of the shepherds, and worship of the wise men.

Close the door of hate and open the door of love all over the world. Let kindness come with every gift and good desires with every greeting. Deliver us from evil by the blessing which Christ brings, and teach us to be merry with clear hearts.

May the Christmas morning make us happy to be children, and Christmas evening bring us to our beds with grateful thoughts, forgiving and forgiven for Jesus' sake.

Tracy Macon Sumner

Father, during the Christmas season, it is so easy to become overly focused on the tradition and the busyness of preparing to celebrate with our family and friends. We thank you for what Christmas means to us and our families, but we ask you to help us stop to think about what it really means: the birth of our dear Savior!

Gerard Manley Hopkins

Moonless darkness stands between.
Past, the Past, no more be seen!
But the Bethlehem-star may lead me
To the sight of Him Who freed me
From the self that I have been.
Make me pure, Lord: You are holy;
Make me meek, Lord: You were lowly;
Now beginning, and always:
Now begin, on Christmas day.

Short Memos to God

"Glory to God in the highest heaven, and peace on earth to all whom God favors." (Luke 2:14)
—Angels at the announcement of the birth of Jesus

Christopher Smart

Where is this stupendous stranger?
Prophets, shepherds, kings, advise.
Lead me to my Master's manger,
show me where my Savior lies.
O Most Mighty! O Most Holy!
Far beyond the seraph's thought:
art thou then so weak and lowly
as unheeded prophets taught?

O the magnitude of meekness!
Worth from worth immortal sprung;
O the strength of infant weakness,
if eternal is so young!
God all-bounteous, all-creative,
whom no ills from good dissuade,
is incarnate, and a native
of the very world he made.

The *Book of Common Prayer*

Almighty God, who has given us your only begotten Son to take our nature upon him—and as at this time to be born of a pure virgin: grant that we, being regenerate and made your children of adoption and grace, may daily be renewed by the Holy Spirit, through our Lord Jesus Christ, who lives and reigns with you and the same Spirit, ever one God.

Prayer of the Victorines

What is this jewel that is so precious? I can see it has been quarried not by men, but by God. It is you, dear Jesus. You have been dug from the rocks of heaven itself to be offered to me as a gift beyond price. You shine in the darkness. Every color of the rainbow can be seen within you. The whole Earth is bathed in your light. Infant Jesus, by being born as man you have taken upon yourself the pain of death. But such a jewel can never be destroyed. You are immortal. And by defying your own death, you shall deliver me from death.

Short Memos to God

Loving God, we give thanks for the birth of your Son Jesus Christ, both in human form in Bethlehem and in spiritual form in our hearts. May he reign as king within every human heart, so that every town and village can live according to his joyful law of love.

—Thomas Münzer

Prayer for Midnight Christmas Mass

Good and gracious God, on this holy night you gave us your Son. The Lord of the universe, wrapped in swaddling clothes, the Savior of all, lying in a manger. On this holy night draw us into the mystery of your love. Join our voices with the heavenly host, that we may sing your glory on high. Give us a place among the shepherds, that we may find the one for whom we have waited. Jesus Christ, your Word made flesh, who lives and reigns with you in the unity of the Holy Spirit in the splendor of eternal light. God forever and ever.

James S. Bell Jr.

Lord Jesus, we thank you that you, the eternal Word of God, became flesh and dwelt among us. Thank you for the Nativity celebration, that you identified with all our joys and sorrows and revealed your Father to us. You, who are the exact representation of the unapproachable God shared his message with us and were able to remain fully God while becoming fully man. Thank you for the signs around us that remind us of you—the Christmas tree pointed toward heaven and the lights that remind us that you are the light of the world.

Short Memos to God

As on this day we keep the special memory of our redeemer's entry into the city, so grand, Lord, that now and ever he may triumph in our hearts. Let the king of grace and glory enter in, and let us lay ourselves and all we are in full joyful homage before him.

—H. C. G. Moule

John Chrysostom

On this day of Christmas, the Word of God, being truly God, appeared in the form of a man, and turned all adoration to himself and away from competing claims for our attention. To him, then, who through the forest of lies has beaten a clear path for us, to Christ, to the Father, and to the Holy Spirit, we offer all praise, now and forever.

Ambrose of Milan

Our God, who looked at us when we had fallen down into death and resolved to redeem us by the arrival of your only begotten Son, grant, we beg you, that those who confess his glorious Incarnation may also be admitted to the fellowship of their redeemer, through the same Jesus Christ our Lord.

Short Memos to God

"Praise God! Bless the one who comes in the name of the Lord! Bless the coming kingdom of our ancestor David! Praise God in highest heaven!" (Mark 11:9–10)

"Behold the Savior of Mankind," by Samuel Wesley

Behold the Savior of mankind
Nailed to the shameful tree!
How vast the love that him inclined
To bleed and die for thee!

Hark, how he groans! while nature shakes,
And earth's strong pillars bend;
The temple's veil in sunder breaks,
The solid marbles rend.

'Tis done! the precious ransom's paid,
"Receive my soul," he cries!
See where he bows his sacred head!
He bows his head, and dies!

But soon he'll break death's envious chain,
And in full glory shine:
O Lamb of God! was ever pain,
Was ever love, like thine?

Thank God It's "Good" Friday!

On the Friday before Easter Sunday, Christians around the world have for centuries recognized "Good Friday," the day the death of Christ on the cross is commemorated. That event, which is central to the Christian faith, has been the focus of literally thousands of writings, prayers, hymns, and poems of gratitude (certainly more than we can list in this book) to God for sending His son, Jesus Christ, to die for the sins of humankind.

Jesus himself uttered one of the best-known Good Friday prayers of all time when he was alone in the Garden of Gethsemane and prayed, "My Father! If it is possible, let this cup of suffering be taken away from me. Yet I want your will, not mine. … My Father! If this cup cannot be taken away until I drink it, your will be done." (Matthew 26:39, 42)

Christians throughout the centuries have recognized the agony Jesus endured as he was arrested, tried, and executed on a cross of wood, and many have penned beautiful prayers and poems to God. Here are just a few examples.

Short Memos to God

Jesus, you let your side be opened by the spear so that there came forth blood and water, wound my heart with the spear of charity so that I may be made worthy of your sacraments which flow from your most holy side.

—Ludolf of Saxony

Mary Elizabeth Coleridge

Good Friday in my heart! Fear and affright!
My thoughts are the Disciples when they fled,
My words are the words that priest and soldier said,
My deed the spear to desecrate the dead.
And day, thy death therein, is changed to night.

Then Easter in my heart sends up the sun.
My thoughts are Mary, when she turned to see.
My words are Peter, answering, 'Lov'st thou Me?
My deeds are all Thine own drawn close to Thee,
And day and night, since Thou dost rise, are one.

Frederick William Faber

My God! my God! and can it be
That I should sin so lightly now,
And think no more of evil thoughts
Than of the wind that waves the bough?

I sin, and Heav'n and earth go round,
As if no dreadful deed were done;
As if Thy blood had never flowed
To hinder sin, or to atone.

I walk the earth with lightsome step,
Smile at the sunshine, breathe the air,
Do my own will, not ever heed
Gethsemane and Thy long prayer.

Shall it be always thus, O Lord?
Wilt Thou not work this hour in me
The grace of Thy Passion merited,
Hatred of self, and love of Thee!

O by the pains of Thy pure love,
Grant me the gift of holy fear;
And by Thy woes and bloody sweat
Wash Thou my guilty conscience clear!

Ever when tempted, make me see,
Beneath the olives' moon pierced shade,
My God, alone, outstretched, and bruised,
And bleeding, on the earth He made;

And make me feel it was my sin,
As though no other sins there were,
That was to Him Who bears the world
A load that He could scarcely bear.

Jeremy Taylor

Blessed be your name, Jesus, Son of the most high God. Blessed be the
sorrow you suffered when your holy hands and feet were nailed to the
tree. Blessed be your love when, the purpose of your pain was accomplished, you gave your soul into the hands of the Father. By your cross
and precious blood you purchased the entire world—all needy souls
since departed and numberless unborn—you who now lives and reigns
in the glory of the eternal Trinity forever and ever.

>< **Short Memos to God**

Lord, thank you that you suffered for the sins of the world.
But thank you even more that you suffered just for me!
May I never forget to tell you how grateful I am for what
you've done for me.

—Tracy Macon Sumner

Bonaventure

Lord, holy Father, show us what kind of man it is who is hanging for our sakes on the cross, whose suffering causes the rocks themselves to crack and crumble with compassion, whose death brings the dead back to life. Let my heart crack and crumble at the sight of him. Let my soul break apart with compassion for his suffering. Let it be shattered with grief at my sins for which he dies. And finally, let it be softened with devoted love for him.

Francis of Assisi

Almighty and eternal God, merciful Father, who has given to the human race your beloved Son as an example of humility, obedience, and patience, to precede us on the way of life, bearing the cross: graciously grant that we be inflamed by his infinite love so that we may take up the sweet yoke of his gospel, following him as his true disciples, so that we shall one day gloriously rise with him and joyfully hear the final sentence: "Come, you blessed of my Father, and possess the kingdom which was prepared for you from the beginning," where you reign with the Son and the Holy Ghost, and where we hope to reign with you, world without end.

Short Memos to God

"Father, forgive these people, because they don't know what they are doing."

—Jesus from the cross (Luke 23:34)

Bernard of Clairvaux

You taught us, Lord, that the greatest love a man can show is to lay down his life for his friends. But your love was even greater than that, because you laid down your life for your enemies. It was while we were still enemies that you brought us back together with you through your death. What other love has there ever been—or ever could be—like yours? You suffered unjustly for the sake of the unjust. You died at the hands of sinners for the sake of the sinful. You became a slave to tyrants to set the oppressed free.

French Prayer

Christ on the cross cries: my people, what have I done to you? What good have I not done for you? Listen to me. Is it nothing to you, all you who pass me by? Look and see if there is any sorrow like my sorrow. We adore you, Jesus Christ, and we bless you, because by your holy cross you have saved the world.

Short Memos to God

Grant, Lord, that in your wounds I may find my safety, in your stripes my cure, in your pain my peace, in your cross my victory, in your resurrection my triumph.

—Jeremy Taylor

Gregory the Great

Lord, you received countless insults from your blasphemers, yet every day you set captive souls free from the grip of the ancient enemy.

You did not turn away your face from the spit of betrayal, yet you wash souls in saving waters.

You accepted your flogging without complaint, yet through your consideration you deliver us from endless punishments.

You endured terrible treatment of all kinds, yet you want to allow us to share in the angels' songs of praise in eternal glory.

You did not refuse to be crowned with thorns, yet you save us from the wounds of sin.

In your thirst you accepted the bitterness of gall, yet you prepare yourself to fill us with eternal delights.

You kept silence under the mocking sent your way by those who crucified you, yet you plead our cases before the Father even though you are his equal in holiness.

You came to taste death, yet you were the Life who came to bring it to the dead.

Easter: The Day the Christian Faith Was Born

Christians believe that Jesus was born of a virgin, that he lived a sinless life on earth, and that he was crucified. But at the very heart of Christianity is the belief that Jesus rose from the dead on the third day after dying on the cross.

Just as Jesus' birth and death are celebrated by Christians around the world, so is his resurrection from the dead. And just as his birth and death have been the subject of many, many prayers throughout the ages, so is his resurrection.

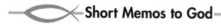 **Short Memos to God**

Lord, help us to be the kind of Christians who present not just the death of Jesus Christ on the cross, but those who serve a risen Lord.

—Tracy Macon Sumner

Martin Luther

Almighty God, who through the death of your Son has destroyed sin and death and by his resurrection has restored the innocence and everlasting life so we could be saved from the power of the devil, and so our mortal bodies raised up from the dead: grant that we may confidently and wholeheartedly believe this message and that, finally, share with your saints in the joyful resurrection of those who have been justified through you.

The Victorines

I see flames of orange, yellow and red shooting upwards to the sky, piercing the whole clouds. I see the clouds themselves chasing the flames upwards, and I feel the air itself reaching for the heavens.

Down below I see great, gray rocks beating against the earth, as if they were pushing their way down to hell.

At your resurrection that which is light and good rises up with you, and that which is heavy and evil is pushed downward.

At your resurrection goodness breaks from evil, life breaks free from death.

Gregory the Great

It is only right, with all the powers of our heart and mind, to praise you, Father, and your only begotten Son, our Lord Jesus Christ. Dear Father, you lovingly and kindly reached down to us, your servants, and gave up your Son. Dear Jesus, you paid for us the debt for Adam's sin to the eternal Father by lovingly and kindly pouring out your blood. You took away the darkness of sin through your wonderful and radiant resurrection. You broke the bonds of death and rose from the grave as a conqueror. You reconciled heaven and earth. Our life had no hope of eternal happiness before you bought us back. Your resurrection has washed away our sins, restored our innocence, and brought us joy. Your love is valuable beyond measure!

We ask you, Lord, to allow your servants to peacefully enjoy this Easter happiness. We ask this through Jesus Christ our Lord, who lives and rules with God the Father, in the unity of the Holy Spirit, forever and ever.

**Short Memos to God**

O God, who for our redemption gave your only-begotten Son to the death of the cross, and by his glorious resurrection delivered us from the power of our enemy: Grant us so to die daily to sin, that we may evermore live with him in the joy of his resurrection.

—Anglican Easter prayer

Hippolytus

Christ is Risen: The world below lies desolate
Christ is Risen: The spirits of evil are fallen
Christ is Risen: The angels of God are rejoicing
Christ is Risen: The tombs of the dead are empty
Christ is Risen indeed from the dead,
the first of the sleepers,
Glory and power are his forever and ever.

A Resurrection-Day Celebration

(By Tracy Macon Sumner)

"I know you are looking for Jesus, who was crucified. He isn't here! He has been raised from the dead, just as he said would happen." (Matthew 28:5–6)

Although it is good for the believer to celebrate and meditate on the birth, life, and death of Christ, we must never forget that at the very heart of our faith is the fact that three days after Jesus died a horrible death on a cross of wood, he was raised from the dead.

That is what the Apostle Paul, the man God assigned the responsibility of taking the gospel of Jesus to the Gentile world, was talking about when he wrote, "If Christ was not raised, then all our preaching is useless, and your trust in God is useless." (1 Corinthians 15:14)

In other words, when it comes to the Christian faith, Jesus' crucifixion and resurrection go hand in hand. You truly can't celebrate one without celebrating the other.

And as believers, we get to celebrate both!

Charles Haddon Spurgeon, one of the greatest evangelists of all time, said of the wonder of Jesus' resurrection from the dead:

"Come, see the place where the Lord lay," with joy and gladness. He does not lie there now. Weep, when you see the tomb of Christ, but rejoice because it is empty. Your sin killed him, but his divinity raised him up. You guilt has murdered him, but his righteousness has restored him. He has hath burst the bonds of death, he has ungirt the cerements of the tomb and has come out more than conqueror, crushing death beneath his feet. Rejoice, Christian, for he is not there—he is risen.

On Good Friday, we celebrate God's demonstration of his incredible love for humankind in giving up his son to die on the cross.

On Easter Sunday, we celebrate his incredible power—power over sin and power over death.

Jesus died so our sins could be forgiven, and he rose from the dead so death could be defeated—both once and for all!

Chapter 15

Prayers for Specific Life Events

Life, especially life for the believer, can be seen as a series of events orchestrated by God to bring us to a point where we are ready to meet in person with Him in heaven.

All of us go through events in life that help define who we are in Christ. From simple and enjoyable events such as birthdays and anniversaries, to those "defining" spiritual moments such as baptism and marriage, to those most difficult times, such as the loss of a loved one, life offers many opportunities for believers to go to God in prayer.

This chapter is devoted to those very special moments in the life of the believer. Some of these prayers are in celebration, some ask for assistance for coming days, and some are devotions to God and to one another.

Birthdays

For the believer, birthdays are a recognition of another year passed in service to God, as well as a time when we can "rededicate" ourselves to following his leading and guiding in the coming year.

The *Gelasian Sacramentary*

Almighty and everlasting God, the maker of all creation: mercifully hear our prayers and grant many and happy years to your servant whose birthday it is, that he may spend all his life so as to please you, through Jesus Christ our Lord.

Short Memos to God

Father, thank you for the blessings of another year of knowing and serving you. I pray that you enable me through your Spirit to be an even better servant in the coming year.

—Tracy Macon Sumner

William Edward Scudamore

Eternal Father, the giver of life, who on this day caused your servant to be born into this world: we thank you, Lord, for all your mercies granted to him from that time until now, and we humbly ask you to continue your gracious favor and protection until his life's end. Help him in every time of trial, shield him in danger, relieve and comfort him in trouble, assist him against temptation, defend him from the assaults of the enemy, so that his days here may pass in peace so that when he dies, he may attain unto the everlasting rest that remains for your people.

Baptism

Baptism is the landmark event in the life of the Christian. It is an outward show of an inward transformation, and also an expression of identification with the life, death, and resurrection of Jesus Christ.

Eastern Orthodox Baptismal

Make yourself manifest, Lord, in this water and grant to him who is baptized in it so to be transformed that he may put off the old man, which is corrupted by deceitful lusts, and may put on the new man, which is formed fresh according to the image of the Creator. Grafted through baptism into the likeness of your death, may he become a partaker also in your resurrection. May he guard the gift of your Holy Spirit, may he increase in the measure of grace, which has been entrusted to him, and may he receive the prize which is God's calling to life above, being numbered among the first born whose names are written in heaven.

Short Memos to God

Thank you, Father, that you have sent your Son, Jesus Christ, to identify with me so that I could have eternal life with you. I know identify with his life, death, and resurrection through baptism into your holy family.

—Tracy Macon Sumner

Egbert of York

Look down from heaven, Lord, upon your flock and your lambs. Bless their bodies and their souls, and grant that those who have received the sign of the cross on their foreheads at baptism may be shown to belong to you on the day of judgment, through Jesus Christ our Lord.

Miles Coverdale

Almighty and eternal God, most merciful Father, as the just live by faith and as it is impossible for anyone to please you without faith, we pray that you will grant to this child the gift of faith, in which you will seal and assure his heart in the Holy Spirit, according to the promise of your Son; that the inner regeneration of the Spirit may be truly represented by the outward baptism, and that the child may be buried with Christ into death and be raised up from death by Christ, to the praise of your glory and the building up of his neighbor.

Stanley Hauerwas

Lord of the Flood, wash us with your Spirit that we may be your ark of life, your peace in the sea of violence. Water is life; water cleans; water kills. Frightened, we are tempted to make a permanent home on the ark. But you force us to seek dry ground. We can do so only because you have taught us to cling to our baptisms, when we are drowned and reborn by the water and fire of your Spirit. So reborn, make us unafraid. Amen.

The Celebration of Baptism

(By Tracy Macon Sumner)

"Anyone who believes and is baptized will be saved." (Mark 16:16)

There are within Christianity differing views on water baptism and whether it is necessary for eternal salvation. Some believe it is an outward sign of what has already happened—namely being "born again" and having our sins forgiven—whereas others believe it is a necessary step in having our sins forgiven in the first place.

What almost all believers agree on when it comes to baptism is the fact that it is a step of obedience for the believer in which he or she publicly identifies with the life, death, and resurrection of Jesus Christ. That is what the Apostle Paul was talking about when he wrote, "Have you forgotten that when we became Christians and were baptized to become one with Christ Jesus, we died with him? For we died and were buried with Christ by baptism. And just as Christ was raised from the dead by the glorious power of the Father, now we also may live new lives." (Romans 6:3–4)

When we are immersed in the water during baptism, it represents the death and burial of Christ and our identification with it. It represents the death of our old sin natures and the beginning of a new life in Christ. It marks the beginning of a new relationship with God through Jesus Christ.

There is no doubt that water baptism is an important step of obedience for all believes to take. But in and of itself, baptism doesn't mean anything unless it is accompanied by the inward transformation Jesus came to perform in everyone who puts their faith in him.

The believer needs to be baptized. But we should never see baptism as something we *have* to do in order to be saved. Rather, we should see it as something we *get* to do because we have put our faith in Jesus Christ for our salvation. We should approach baptism as both an act of obedience and as a celebration of the new life we have received in Christ when we are born again.

Weddings

God didn't create marriage as just an expression of love between a man and a woman, or to provide children with loving families. Marriage is also a metaphor for the love of God for humankind, in that he gives us the very best he has, including his own Son, Jesus Christ.

Weddings are celebrations of the love between a man and a woman who have pledged to live their lives together. But they are also solemn events in which they take vows in front of God and in front of their family and friends to love one another for a lifetime.

Here are some well-known and not-so-well-known wedding prayers.

Roman Catholic Wedding Prayer

Almighty God, hear our prayers for [Groom] and [Bride] who have come here today to be united in the sacrament of marriage. Increase their faith in you and in each other, and through them bless your church. We ask this through our Lord Jesus Christ, your Son, who lives and reigns with you and the Holy Spirit, one God, forever and ever.

Roman Catholic Prayer of Bride and Groom

Lord Jesus, grant that I and my spouse may have a true and understanding love for each other. Grant that we may both be filled with faith and trust. Give us the grace to live with each other in peace and harmony. May we always bear with one another's weaknesses and grow from each other's strengths. Help us to forgive one another's failings and grant us patience, kindness, cheerfulness and the spirit of placing the well-being of one another ahead of self.

May the love that brought us together grow and mature with each passing year. Bring us both ever closer to you through our love for each other. Let our love grow to perfection. Amen.

Roman Catholic Shorter Nuptial Blessing

Be appeased, O Lord, by our humble prayers, and in your kindness assist this institution of marriage which you have ordained for the propagation of the human race; so that this union made here, joined by your authority, may be preserved by your help. Through the same our Lord Jesus Christ, your Son, who lives and reigns with you in the unity of the Holy Spirit, God, world without end. Amen.

Short Memos to God

The Lord sanctify and bless you, the Lord pour the riches of his grace upon you, that you may please him and live together in holy love to your lives' end. Amen.

—John Knox's wedding prayer

A Father's Wedding Prayer (Anonymous)

This is the best dowry of hopes, wishes and prayers I would be able to offer:

May God give you the grace of wit and wisdom to understand that rainbows are only the result of showers, dust, and hope. May you always have joy in the morning and trust in the evening, and may your sorrows be short and without scars.

May your lives have a spirit neither bent by belligerence nor broken by failure; may you simply love each other. May you share with each other spring flowers, dirty dishes, music, rain, death, mushrooms, a measure of boredom, strawberries, and God.

May that God never make you immune to the wonderful afflictions of real love, making you instead farsighted to each other's faults, tongue-tied to criticism, and short of memory to petty hurts and slights.

May God provide the confidence and serenity that comes only from the assurance of each other's fidelity and the tolerance, as years go by, of wrinkles and gray hairs, short tempers, curlers, and Monday mornings.

May no one steal from you laughter at the top of the stairs or giggles and whispers in a dark room. May you keep a hunger for each other, the appetite to taste tomorrow, and deep knowledge of and devotion to your past, heritage and families.

May you perpetuate trust, the radiation of vitality, kind answers to sharp questions and sharp humor to unkind attitudes. May your fights be fierce and short, and may each truce be warm and long and held in each other's arms before the sun comes up.

May you walk with wise men, sing loud songs at late hours, share secrets, have healthy children, and provide smiles for lonesome strangers and prayers for those without hope.

May you never forget small things; smiles, birthdays, holding hands, family, old friends, the neglected, and the simplicity of saying please and thank you.

May you keep a warm, generous, and happy house where love is the insulation and God is present. May your children be friends of God's child, Jesus. May your union bring a smile to the face of the Holy Spirit, and may he live in your pots and pans, in your hope and aspirations.

The Church of Ireland's *Family Prayer Book*

God, bless your servants who are about to be joined together this day in holy matrimony. Keep them, we humbly ask you, under the protection of your good providence, and make them to have a perpetual fear and love of thy holy name. Look, Lord, mercifully upon them from heaven, and bless them, that they obeying your will and always being in safety under your protection, may abide in your love until their lives' end.

A Celtic Wedding Blessing

May the light of friendship guide your paths together.
May the laughter of children grace the halls of your home.
May the joy of living for one another trip a smile from your lips, a twinkle from your eye.
And when eternity beckons,
at the end of a life heaped high with love,
May the good Lord embrace you
with the arms that have nurtured you
the whole length of your joy-filled days.

Short Memos to God

That I may come near to her, draw me nearer to you than to her. That I may know her, make me to know you more than her. That I may love her with the love of a perfectly whole heart, cause me to love you more than her and most of all.

—Temple Gairdner of Cairo, before his marriage

At Times of Loss (Bereavement)

Few times in life move us to prayer more than the loss of a loved one or a good friend. Death is completely final, in that we will never again enjoy that person's presence in a physical sense. Prayers associated with death are some of the most heart-rending, honest prayers we can utter. They are said at times when our emotions are raw and times when we need to hear from God.

Edward White Benson (on the Death of His Young Son)

O God, to me who am left to mourn his departure, grant that I may not sorrow as one without hope for my beloved who sleeps in you; but as always remembering his courage, and the love that united us on earth, I may begin again with new courage to serve you more fervently who are the only source of true love and true fortitude that when I have passed a few more days in this valley of tears and this shadow of death, supported by your rod and staff, I may see him face to face, in those pastures and beside those waters of comfort where I believe he already walks with you. O Shepherd of the sheep, have pity on this darkened soul of mine.

The Roman Catholic *Family Prayer Book*

Father, God of all consolation, in your unending love and mercy for us you turn the darkness of death into the dawn of new life.

Show compassion to your people in their sorrow, be our refuge and our strength, to lift us from the darkness of this grief to the peace and light of your presence.

Your Son, our Lord Jesus Christ, by dying for us, conquered death and by rising again, restored life. May we then go forward eagerly to meet him, and after our life on earth be reunited with our brothers and sisters where every tear will be wiped away. We ask this through Christ our Lord. Amen.

Short Memos to God

Ah, poor lonely widow and miserable woman that I am, may he who does not forsake widows and orphans console me. O my God, console me! O my Jesus, strengthen me in my weakness!

—Elizabeth of Hungary, after the death of her husband

Charles Wesley

I feel a strong immortal hope,
Which bears my mournful spirit up
Beneath its mountain load;
Redeemed from death, and grief, and pain,
I soon shall find my friend again
Within the arms of God.

Pass a few fleeting moments more
And death the blessing shall restore
Which death has snatched away;
For me You will the summons send,
And give me back my parted friend
In that eternal day.

Short Memos to God

Into your hands, Lord, we commend the spirit of our loved one, now passing from us into your eternal presence. Lord Jesus, receive him into your holy keeping.

—Queen Elizabeth I

Thomas Moore

Come, you disconsolate, wherever you languish,
come to the mercy seat, fervently kneel.
Here bring your wounded hearts, here tell your anguish:
Earth has no sorrow that heaven cannot heal.

Joy of the desolate, light of the straying,
hope of the penitent, fadeless and pure!
Here speaks the Comforter, tenderly saying,
"Earth has no sorrow that heaven cannot cure."

Here see the Bread of Life; see waters flowing
forth from the throne of God, pure from above.
Come to the feast of love; come, ever knowing
Earth has no sorrow but heaven can remove.

Horatio Gates Spafford (on the Tragic Death of His Four Daughters)

When peace like a river, attends my way;
When sorrows like sea billows roll;
Whatever my lot, you have taught me to say,
It is well, it is well with my soul.

It is well ... with my soul. It is well, it is well, with my soul.

Though Satan should buffet, though trials should come,
Let this blest assurance control,
That Christ has regarded my helpless estate,
And has shed His own blood for my soul.

It is well ... with my soul. It is well, it is well, with my soul.

He lives—oh, the bliss of this glorious thought;
My sin, not in part, but the whole,
Is nailed to the cross, and I bear it no more.
Praise the Lord, praise the Lord, Oh my soul.

Funeral Prayer

May he be with God. May he be with the living God. May he be with
the immortal God. May he be in God's hands. May he be where the
great name of God is. May he be where God's greatness is. May he be
with the living God now and on the day of judgment. Live in God, live
in eternal delight.

Short Memos to God

Grant, Lord, that the soul of our brother here departed
may rest in your peace and protection, and reign in your
kingdom in heaven.

—Martin J. Routh

John Henry Newman

Go forth upon your journey, Christian soul!
Go from this world! Go, in the Name of God
The Omnipotent Father, Who created you!
Go, in the Name of Jesus Christ, our Lord,
Son of the Living God, Who bled for you!
Go, in the Name of the Holy Spirit,
Who has been poured out on you!
Go in the name
Of Angels and Archangels; in the name
Of Thrones and Dominations; in the name
Of Princedoms and of Powers; and in the name
Of Cherubim and Seraphim, go forth!
Go, in the name of Patriarchs and Prophets;
And of Apostles and Evangelists,
Of Martyrs and Confessors, in the name
Of holy Monks and Hermits; in the name
Of holy Virgins; and all Saints of God,

Both men and women, go! Go on your course;
And may your place today be found in peace,
And may your dwelling be the Holy Mount
Of Zion: through the Same, through Christ our Lord.

Funeral Day Prayer (Anonymous)

Lord Jesus Christ, I come to you at the beginning of this day, in all my loneliness and uncertainty I come. I thank you for all those who will be sharing the day with me, for the minister, relatives and friends, and all those who have been so helpful. Help me not to worry about the arrangements which have been made, about the visitors who will be coming, about my fear of emotion, about the service, about the weather. I bring this day to you, help me in my weakness to prove your strength.

Tracy Macon Sumner

Lord, your Word tells us of a friend who sticks closer than a brother. That is just the kind of friend I have lost today. Only you can truly understand the sorrow I feel over his sudden and tragic death, and only you can understand what his friendship meant and still means to me. As I grieve over his parting, I ask you to remind me daily of the blessing you gave me when you allowed me to know him as more than a friend, but also as a brother.

Death Has Been Defeated

(Adapted from the writings of Charles Haddon Spurgeon)

"... only by dying could he [Jesus] break the power of the Devil, who has the power of death." (Hebrews 2:14)

For the believer, death has lost its sting because the devil's power over it has been destroyed. For that reason, we shouldn't fear death but instead ask for the grace of God the Holy Spirit that in knowing well and firmly believing in the death of our Redeemer, you may be strengthened when you are faced with death.

Living near the cross of Calvary, you may think of death with pleasure, and welcome it when it comes with intense delight. It is sweet to die in the Lord: it is a covenant-blessing to sleep in Jesus. Death is no longer banishment, it is a return from exile, a going home to the many mansions where the loved ones already dwell. The distance between glorified spirits in heaven and militant saints on Earth seems great; but it is not so. We are not far from home—a moment will bring us there. The sail is spread; the soul is launched upon the deep. How long will be its voyage? How many wearying winds must beat upon the sail until it shall be reefed in the port of peace? How long shall that soul be tossed upon the waves before it comes to that sea which knows no storm? Listen to the answer, "Absent from the body, present with the Lord."

Your ship has just departed, but it is already at its haven. It did but spread its sail and it was there. Like that ship of old, upon the Lake of Galilee, a storm had tossed it, but Jesus said, "Peace, be still," and immediately it came to land. Think not that a long period intervenes between the instant of death and the eternity of glory. When the eyes close on Earth they open in heaven. The horses of fire are not an instant on the road. Then, child of God, what is there for you to fear in death, seeing that through the death of your Lord its curse and sting are destroyed, and now it is but a Jacob's ladder whose foot is in the dark grave, but its top reaches to glory everlasting.

Chapter 16

Prayers for Morning, Meals, and Bedtime

If there are three things we all do each and every day, it's getting up to face the day, eating, and going to sleep at night. Most believers know that some of the best times to pray are in the morning, over meals, and at bedtime. For that reason, Christian tradition and history includes countless prayers suited for just those times.

This chapter contains many of those prayers and blessings, and they give us good models for prayer during those everyday life events.

Arising and Meeting with God

Jesus himself set an example of the importance of starting the day off with prayer. In several passages of the gospels, we read that Jesus got up early, sat by himself, and prayed. No doubt, Jesus talked to his heavenly Father about what he was going to be doing that day, asking for his power and direction for the day ahead. We should do the very same. Here are some examples of how we can do just that.

Orthodox Prayer Book

How good it is to give thanks to you, Lord, and to sing praises to your glorious name; to declare your loving kindness at the break of the day, and your faithfulness during the night. Lord, hear our voices at the dawn of the day, and in the morning let us be found ready by you. Lord, forgive and pardon all our sins. Holy One, overshadow your right hand upon us, and heal all our infirmities for the sake of your eternal name.

Short Memos to God

Now I awake and see the light;
Lord, You have kept me through the night.
To You I lift my voice and pray
That You will keep me through the day.
If I should die before 'tis done,
O God, accept me through Your Son!
Amen.

—Traditional children's morning prayer

Robert Collyer

Most holy and ever-loving God, we thank you once more for the quiet rest of the night that has gone by, for the new promise that has come with this fresh morning, and for hope of this day. While we have slept, the world in which we live has swept on, and we have rested under the shadow of your love. May we trust you this day for all the needs of the body, the soul, and the spirit. Give us this day our daily bread.

John Henry Jowett

Our Father, may we walk as your children today. May the sense of our relationship with you fill us with a saving self-respect. May our lives be as glorious as our relationship. May we walk as children of God, through Jesus Christ our Lord.

James S. Bell Jr.

Lord, your Word says that your mercies are new every morning. We awake to your renewed covenant that you never leave us or forsake us and that your forgiveness and grace have not lessened. You never change in your love for us, and we pray that we will not miss the great blessings in store for us through the merits of your son, Jesus Christ. May we go forth this day clothed with the full armor of God to protect us from evil and a deep desire to keep your commandments and fulfill your purposes for our lives. As your Word says, "This is the day the Lord has made; we will rejoice and be glad in it." Let the joy of your presence pervade our lives as we pray and read your Word this morning.

Our Morning Nourishment

(By Tracy Macon Sumner)

"The next morning Jesus awoke long before daybreak and went out alone into the wilderness to pray." (Mark 1:35)

There are several instances recorded in the four gospels where Jesus got up early in the morning and went to a private place to pray.

At first, it might be tempting to think that Jesus prayed early in the morning because it was the only time he could get away from everyone. But there was more to it than that. In fact, there is Old Testament precedence for the practice of arising early to pray. For example, King David wrote:

- ◆ "Listen to my voice in the morning, Lord. Each morning I bring my requests to you and wait expectantly." (Psalm 5:3)

- ◆ "But as for me, I will sing about your power. I will shout with joy each morning because of your unfailing love. For you have been my refuge, a place of safety in the day of distress." (Psalm 59:16)

- ◆ "Let me hear of your unfailing love to me in the morning, for I am trusting you. Show me where to walk, for I have come to you in prayer." (Psalm 143:8)

Jesus prayed early in the morning partly because it was one of the few times in the day where he could have any privacy. But more important, he did it because it was a perfect time for him to be alone with his Father and "energize" himself for the work that lay ahead that day.

Today, experts on diet and nutrition tell us that even those who are attempting to lose weight should never neglect a good breakfast. In the morning, they tell us, it is vital to nourish the body for the day ahead.

The very same thing is true in our spiritual lives. It is important to pray at all times, but it may well be that there is no more important time of the day to get alone with God and pray than in the morning.

The *Book of Common Prayer*

Lord our heavenly Father, almighty and everlasting God who has safely brought us to the beginning of this day: defend us in the same with your mighty power and grant that this day we fall into no sin or run into any kind of danger. Rather, let all our doings be ordered by your authority, and help us to do what is righteous in your sight—through Jesus Christ our Lord.

St. Patrick's "Breastplate"

I arise today through a mighty strength, the invocation of the Trinity, through the belief in the threeness, through confession of the oneness of the Creator of Creation.

I arise today through the strength of Christ's birth with his baptism, through the strength of his crucifixion with his burial, through the strength of his resurrection with his ascension, through the strength of his descent for the judgment of Doom.

I arise today through the strength of the love of Cherubim, in obedience of angels, in the service of archangels, in hope of resurrection to meet with reward, in prayers of patriarchs, in predictions of prophets, in preaching of apostles, in faith of confessors, in innocence of holy virgins, in deeds of righteous men.

I arise today through the strength of heaven: Light of sun, radiance of moon, splendor of fire, speed of lightning, swiftness of wind, depth of sea, stability of earth, firmness of rock.

I arise today through God's strength to pilot me: God's might to uphold me, God's wisdom to guide me, God's eye to look before me, God's ear to hear me, God's word to speak for me, God's hand to guard me, God's way to lie before me, God's shield to protect me, God's host to save me from snares of devils, from temptations of vices, from everyone who shall wish me ill, far and near, alone and in multitude.

I summon today all these powers between me and those evils, against every cruel merciless power that may oppose my body and soul, against incantations of false prophets, against black laws of pagans, against false laws of heretics, against craft of idolatry, against spells of witches and smiths and wizards, against every knowledge that corrupts man's body and soul.

Christ to shield me today against poison, against burning, against drowning, against wounding, so that there may come to me abundance of reward. Christ with me, Christ before me, Christ behind me, Christ in me, Christ beneath me, Christ above me, Christ on my right, Christ on my left, Christ when I lie down, Christ when I sit down, Christ when I arise, Christ in the heart of every man who thinks of me, Christ in the mouth of everyone who speaks of me, Christ in every eye that sees me, Christ in every ear that hears me.

I arise today through a mighty strength, the invocation of the Trinity, through belief in the threeness, through confession of the oneness, of the Creator of Creation.

Henry Suso

My soul has desired you all night, eternal wisdom! And in the early morning I turn to you from the depths of my heart. May your holy presence remove all dangers from my soul and body. May your many graces fill the deepest recesses of my heart and inflame it with your divine love. Most sweet Jesus, turn your face toward me, for this morning with all the powers of my soul I fly to you and salute you, humbly asking you that the thousands times a thousand angels who minister to you may praise you for me, that the thousand times ten thousand blessed spirits who surround your throne may glorify you for me today.

Short Memos to God

Father, let my first thought today be of you, let my first impulse be to worship you, let my first speech be your name, let my first action be to kneel before you in prayer.

—John Baillie

Celtic Prayer

Come I this day to the Father,
Come I this day to the Son,
Come I to the Holy Spirit powerful;
Come I this day with God,
Come I this day with Christ,
Come I with the Spirit of kindly balm.

God, and Spirit, and Jesus,
From the crown of my head
To the soles of my feet;
Come I with my reputation,
Come I with my testimony,
Come I to you, Jesus;
Jesus, shelter me.

Isaac Watts

God of the morning, at Whose voice
The cheerful sun makes haste to rise,
And like a giant does rejoice
To run his journey through the skies.

From the fair chambers of the east
The circuit of his race begins,
And, without weariness or rest,
Round the whole earth he flies and shines.

O like the sun may I fulfill
The appointed duties of the day,
With ready mind and active will
March on and keep my heavenly way.

But I shall rove and lose the race,
If God, my Sun, should disappear,
And leave me in this world's wild maze,
To follow every wandering star.

Mozarabic Luturgy

Let our prayer, Lord, come to you in the morning. You took upon
yourself our weak and suffering nature. Grant us to pass this day in
gladness and peace, without stumbling and without stain, that, reaching the evening without any temptation, we may praise you, the eternal
King—through your mercy, our God, who is blessed and lives and governs all things, world without end.

Philaret of Moscow

Lord, grant me to greet the coming day in peace and help me in all
things to rely upon your holy will. In every hour of the day reveal your
will to me. Bless my dealings with all who surround me. Teach me to
treat all that comes to throughout the day with peace of soul and with
firm conviction that your will governs all. In all my deeds and words,
guide my thoughts and feelings. In unforeseen events, let me not forget that all are sent by you. Teach me to act firmly and wisely, without
embittering and embarrassing others. Give me strength to bear the
fatigue of the coming day with all that it shall bring. Direct my will,
teach me to pray. And you, yourself, pray in me. Amen.

Short Memos to God

This is the day the Lord has made. We will rejoice and
be glad in it.
—Psalm 118:24

Martin Luther

My heavenly Father, I thank you, through Jesus Christ, your beloved Son, that you kept me safe from all evil and danger last night. I ask you to save me today as well from every evil and sin, so that all I do and the way that I live will please you. I put myself in your care, body and soul, and all that I have. Let your holy angels be with me, so that the evil enemy will not gain power over me.

Thomas Arnold

Lord, grant that my heart may be truly cleansed and filled with your Holy Spirit, and that I may arise to serve you and lie down to sleep in entire confidence in you, submitting to your will, ready for life or for death. Let me live for the day, not overly concerned with worldly cares, but feeling that my treasure is not here, and desiring truly to be joined to you in your heavenly kingdom, and to those who are already gone to you. Lord, save me from sin and guide me with your Spirit and keep me in faithful obedience to you, through Jesus Christ your Son, our Lord.

Basil the Great

As I rise from sleep, I thank you, Holy Trinity, for your loving-kindness and patience. You were not angry with me, even though I am lazy and full of sin. You have not destroyed me for the wrongs I have done. Rather, you have shown unchanging love for me. When I was bowed low in dark despair, you raised me up to sing the morning hymn and glorify your Lordship.

Now give light to the eye of my mind, and open my ears to hear your words and learn your commandments. Help me to obey your will, sing to you with all my heart, and give praise to your holy name, the Father and the Son and the Holy Spirit, now and ever and unto ages of ages.

Greek Church Liturgy

Lord our God, who has chased the slumber from our eyes and once more assembled us to lift up our hands unto you and the praise your just judgments: accept our prayers and prayers and give us faith and love. Bless our coming in and our going out, our thoughts, words, and works, and let us begin this day with the praise of the unspeakable sweetness of your mercy. We honor your name. Your kingdom come, through Jesus Christ our Lord.

Mealtime Blessings

Mealtime blessings—or "saying grace," as so many of us know it—are a big part of Christian tradition. As individuals, friends, and families alike sit down for a meal, they take the time to thank God for their food and for one another. Here are some of those kinds of prayers.

Richard Baxter

Most gracious God, who has given us Christ and with him all that is necessary to life and godliness: we thankfully take this our food as the gift of your bounty and obtained by his merits. Bless it to the nourishment and strength of our frail bodies to help prepare us for cheerful service to you.

Short Memos to God

Bless us, Lord, and these your gifts, which we are about to receive, from thy bounty, through Christ, Our Lord. Amen.

—Traditional table blessing

Celtic Grace Before Food

Dear Lord, bless the food for our use, and us for your service. May the food restore our strength, giving new energy to tired limbs, new thought to weary minds. May the wine restore our souls, giving new visions to dry spirits, new warmth to cold hearts. And once refreshed we offer again our minds and bodies, our hearts and spirits, to proclaim your glory.

John Wesley

Lord my God, I bless your holy name for this mercy, which I have now received from your bounty and goodness. Feed now my soul with your grace, that I may make it my meat and drink to do your gracious will, through Jesus Christ my Savior. Amen.

Tracy Macon Sumner

Lord, I thank you that you so wonderfully and faithfully meet my every need, including the physical need for nourishment. I thank you for this food and drink I am about to receive, and I ask you to use it to keep my body healthy and strong and to strengthen me for your service.

Short Memos to God

God is great and God is good,
and we thank him for our food.
By his hand we must be fed,
give us Lord, our daily bread. Amen.
—Traditional children's mealtime blessing

Evening and Bedtime Prayers

Evening and bedtime are wonderful times for the believer to spend some time talking with God in prayer. It is a time when he or she can thank him for the day past and ask him to bless the sleep that is part of the preparation for the next day.

Robert Louis Stevenson

Lord, behold our family here assembled.
We thank you for this place in which we dwell,
for the love that unites us,
for the peace accorded to us this day,
for the hope with which we expect the morrow;
for the health, the work, the food and the bright skies
that make our lives delightful;
for our friends in all parts of the earth. Amen.

Gaelic Bedtime Prayer

This bed I make in the name of the Father, and of the Son, and of the Holy Spirit. In the name of the night we were conceived, in the name of the day we were baptized, in the name of every night, every day, every season, and of every angel that is in heaven.

Lutheran Manual of Prayer

Abide with us, Lord, for it is toward evening and the day is far spent. Abide with us and with your whole church. Abide with us in the evening of the day, in the evening of life, in the evening of the world. Abide with us and with all your faithful ones, Lord, in time and eternity.

> **Short Memos to God**
>
> Now I lay me down to sleep,
> I pray thee, Lord, thy child to keep:
> Thy love guard me through the night
> And wake me with the morning light.
> Amen.
>
> —Traditional children's bedtime prayer

Archbishop Laud

Lord God, send peaceful sleep to refresh our tired bodies. May your help always renew us and keep us strong in your service. We ask this through Christ our Lord. Into your hands, Lord, we commend our souls and bodies, asking that you keep us this night under your protection and strengthen us for your service tomorrow, for Christ's sake.

Tracy Macon Sumner

Thank you, Lord, for the day past and for this evening. I ask that you will be with me as I sleep, keeping my mind and my soul safe from the attacks of the enemy. I pray that I will have a restful night so that I will be ready to devote another day to you.

Indian Orthodox Bedtime Prayer

Grant us, Lord God, that while our bodies rest from the labors of the day and as our souls are released from the thoughts of this world, we may stand in your presence with tranquility and quietness in this evening hour. Make us worthy to offer you ceaseless praise and thanksgiving without interruption. May we acknowledge your loving-kindness and mercy by which you rule and direct and save our souls. Unto you we offer praise and thanksgiving now and unto ages of ages.

 **Short Memos to God**

Lighten our darkness, we ask you, Lord; we pray: and by your great mercy defend us from all perils and dangers of this night; for the love of your only Son our Savior Jesus Christ. Amen.

—Anglican evening prayer

Thomas Becon

Lord, heavenly Father, by whose divine decree the darkness covers the earth and brings to us bodily rest and quietness: we give you our hearty thanks for the loving-kindness you have shown in preserving us during the past day, and in giving us all things necessary for our health and comfort. And we humbly ask you, for Jesus Christ's sake, to forgive us all the sins we have committed in thought, word, or deed, and that you will shadow us this night under the wings of your almighty power, and defend us from all power of the evil one. May our souls, whether sleeping or awake, wait upon you, delight in you, and evermore praise you, so that when the light of day returns, we may rise with pure and thankful hearts, casting away the works of darkness and putting on the armor of light; through Jesus Christ. Amen.

Henry Vaughan

Abide with us, most blessed and merciful Savior, for it is toward evening and the day is far spent. As long as you are with us, we are in the light. When you are with us all is brightness and sweetness. We talk with you, watch with you, live with you, and lie down with you. Abide then with us, God whom our souls love. Sun of righteousness with healing under your wings, arise in our hearts. Make your light shine in darkness as a perfect day in the dead of night.

Augustine of Hippo

Dear Lord, watch over those who wake, or watch, or weep tonight, and give your angels charge over those who sleep. Tend to your sick ones, Lord Christ. Rest your weary ones, bless your dying ones, soothe your suffering ones, pity your afflicted ones, and shield your joyous ones. Do all this for your love's sake.

Short Memos to God

Keep us, Lord, so awake in the duties of our callings that we may sleep in your peace and wake in your glory.
—John Donne

John Calvin

Merciful God, eternal light, shining in darkness, you who chases away the night of sin and all blindness of heart: since you have appointed the night for rest and the day for work, we ask you to grant that our bodies may rest in peace and quietness, so that afterward they may be able to endure the labor they must bear.

St. Patrick

May your holy angels, O Christ, Son of living God, guard our sleep, our rest, our shining bed. Let them reveal true visions to us in our sleep, O High Prince of the universe, O great king of the mysteries! May no demons, no ill, no calamity or terrifying dreams disturb our rest, our willing, prompt rest. May our watch be holy, our work, our task, our sleep, our rest without let, without break.

The Peace God Gives

(Adapted from the writings of Mary Wilder Tileston)

"May the Lord of peace himself always give you peace no matter what happens." (2 Thessalonians 3:16)

"You hide them in the shelter of your presence." (Psalm 31:20)

It's the small things—just because they *are* so small—that cause us distress and disturb us. I am referring to the weight of daily cares: the small details of personal sacrifice, the careful routine of running a household, the raising of children, dealing with your circle of friends, duties outside the home, private personal matters. Each of these things, in and of themselves, can weigh us down, but when you throw them all together and try to bear them on your shoulders alone, it is sometimes more than you can, in your own strength, bear.

We often feel rushed and tempted to worry. We often place too much importance on ourselves. We may feel overwhelmed with the small details of life. But if we approach those things rightly—as mature Christians should—we can settle down into a warm, bright center of one regular, peaceful, and fruitful endeavor: prayer. Where there is prayer, there is peace. And our God, who makes everything we have to do possible, knows, helps, and cares.

At the end of the day, no matter how many cares, worries, and annoyances may come upon us, we can always have the peace that God gives us, knowing that He's in control, that He cares, and that He has our very best in mind.

Chapter 17

Prayers for Children and Parents

There may be no event in the lives of men and women that move them to pray as much as the birth of a child. Becoming a parent is a huge responsibility, and many of those who become moms and dads know that they will need help from on high to get themselves—as well as their children—through it successfully and safely.

Parents can pray for themselves to become competent—or better—parents through everything parenthood brings to them. They can pray for their own peace of mind as they embark on the long and very often difficult journey of raising a child from infancy through young adulthood. And they can pray that their child will become anything and everything God wants them to be.

In this chapter, we have listed some prayers of parents for their children, as well as some prayers especially for children.

Hannah's Prayer

O Lord Almighty, if you will look down upon my sorrow and answer my prayer and give me a son, then I will give him back to you. He will be yours for his entire lifetime, and as a sign that he has been dedicated to the Lord, his hair will never be cut. (1 Samuel 2:11)

Mother's Prayer

Lord God almighty who has made us out of nothing and redeemed us by the precious blood of your only Son, I humbly ask you to care for the work of your hands and defend both me and the tender fruit of my womb from all perils and evils. I beg you, for myself, your grace, protection, and a happy delivery. For my child, I beg that you would preserve it for baptism, set it aside for yourself, and make it yours forever. Through Jesus Christ your Son, our Lord.

Short Memos to God

Help us to remember that being a father isn't just a blessing but one of the biggest responsibilities with which you can entrust a man. Strengthen all fathers in meeting that responsibility.

—Source unknown

The *Gelasian Sacramentary*

Almighty God, giver of all good things, mercifully behold this your child now going forth in your name to school, so replenish him with the truth of your doctrine and adorn him with innocence of life, that both by word and good example he may faithfully serve you to the glory of your name, and edification of your church, through Jesus Christ our Lord.

James S. Bell Jr.

Father, we thank you that though we are not perfect parents we have you as a model and your Word as our guide in raising godly children.

Let us give completely of ourselves on behalf of these precious lives that you have lent to us for only a short time. Grant us wisdom to bring them up in the reverence and discipline of the Lord, to point them to you at all times. May we model your lavish love and gentle discipline, trying not to control and yet providing them with necessary boundaries. Let us always encourage, instruct, and lead them to make their own wise decisions.

Short Memos to God

Lord, you are a God who helps the helpless. Let all mothers and fathers look to that part of your character as a model when it comes to caring for their children.

—Source unknown

Abigail Van Buren (a.k.a. "Dear Abby")

O heavenly Father, make me a better parent. Teach me to understand my children, to listen patiently to what they have to say, and to answer all their questions kindly.

Keep me from interrupting them or contradicting them. Make me as courteous to them as I would have them be to me. Forbid that I should ever laugh at their mistakes, or resort to shame or ridicule when they displease me.

May I never punish them for my own selfish satisfaction or to show my power. Let me not tempt my child to lie or steal. And guide me hour by hour that I may demonstrate by all I say and do that honesty produces happiness.

Reduce, I pray, the meanness in me. And when I am out of sorts, help me, O Lord, to hold my tongue. May I ever be mindful that my children are children, and I should not expect of them the judgment of adults. Let me not rob them of the opportunity to make decisions.

Bless me with the bigness to grant them all their reasonable requests, and the courage to deny them privileges I know will do them harm. Make me fair and just and kind. And fit me, O Lord, to be loved and respected and imitated by my children. Amen.

Marian Wright Edelman

Dear God, I thank you for the gift of this child to raise, this life to share, this mind to help mold, this body to nurture, and this spirit to enrich. Let me never betray this child's trust, dampen this child's hope, or discourage this child's dreams. Help me, dear God, to help this precious child become all you mean him to be. Let your grace and love fall on him like gentle breezes and give him inner strength and peace and patience for the journey ahead.

Walter Rauschenbach

O God, since you have laid these little children into our arms in utter helplessness and with no protection other than our love, we pray that the sweet appeal of their baby hands may not be in vain. Let no innocent life in our cities be quenched again in useless pain through our ignorance and sin. May we who are mothers and fathers seek eagerly to add wisdom to our love, so that our love won't be deadly because it's not guided by knowledge. Bless the doctors and nurses, and all the friends of men who are giving of their skill and devotion to the care of our children. If there are any who were kissed by love in their own infancy but who have no child to whom they may give as they have received, grant them such largeness of sympathy that they may rejoice to pay their debt in full to all children who have need of them. Forgive us, our Father, for the heartlessness of the past. Grant us great tenderness for all children who suffer, and a growing sense of the divine mystery that is brooding in the soul of every child.

A Child's Prayer for Morning

Now, before I run to play,
Let me not forget to pray
To God who kept me through the night
And waked me with the morning light.
Help me, Lord, to love thee more
Than I ever loved before,
In my work and in my play
Be thou with me through the day.
Amen.

Short Memos to God

God in heaven hear my prayer,
keep me in thy loving care.
Be my guide in all I do,
Bless all those who love me too.
Amen.

—Traditional children's prayer for guidance

Child's Evening Hymn

I hear no voice, I feel no touch,
I see no glory bright;
But yet I know that God is near,
In darkness as in light.
God watches ever by my side,
And hears my whispered prayer:
A God of love for a little child
Both night and day does care.

James S. Bell Jr.

May we protect our children from evil and instruct them thoroughly
in our faith. We pray never to be a stumbling block to their growth.
Give them the grace to be obedient and have friends and role models
who will exemplify integrity. Let us by your Spirit help our children
fully develop their gifts and talents in your service. Most of all may
they embrace you as their Lord and Savior and lover of their souls at an
early stage of their lives. We trust you to complete your plans for their
lives and when they fail or stray, help us not to be harsh but patient and
forgiving, leading them back to the path of truth and righteousness.

William Boyd Carpenter

Lord God, in whose hands are the issues of life, we thank you for your
gifts to us at this time. We thank you for the life given and the life preserved. And as you have knit together life and love in one fellowship, so
we pray and ask you to grant that with this fresh gift of life to us there

may be given an increase of love one to another. Grant that the presence of weakness may awaken our tenderness, enable us to minister to the little one that has been given to us in all lovingness, wisdom, and fidelity. And grant that he may live as your child, and may serve this generation according to your will, through Jesus Christ our Lord.

Short Memos to God

Angel of God, my Guardian dear,
To whom God's love commits me here;
Ever this day, be at my side
To light and guard
To rule and guide.

—Traditional children's prayer for protection

Parents' Prayer

Most loving Father, the example of parenthood, you have entrusted our children to us to bring them up for you and prepare them for everlasting life.

Assist us with your grace, that we may fulfill this sacred duty with competence and love. Teach us what to give and what to withhold. Show us when to reprove, when to praise, and when to be silent.

Make us gentle and considerate, yet firm and watchful. Keep us from the weakness of indulgence and the excess of severity.

Give us the courage to be disliked sometimes by our children when we must do necessary things that are displeasing in their eyes. Give us the imagination to enter their world in order to understand and guide them.

Grant us the virtues we need to lead them by word and example in the ways of wisdom and piety. One day, with them, may we enter into the joys of our true and lasting home with you in heaven.

John Cosin

Almighty God and heavenly Father, we thank you for the children you have given us. Give us grace to train them in your faith, fear, and love, that as they advance in years they may grow in grace, and my hereafter be found in the number of your elect children; through Jesus Christ our Lord.

Working Mother's Prayer

O Lord, since I must now entrust my precious child into the arms of another so that I may go forth to earn bread for our table, accept my offering of tears and deep regret.

Take my child, Lord—and my aching heart—and lay them together in your dear Mother's lap where both may rest secure until I come again to claim my treasures.

Amen.

Short Memos to God

Dear God most high, hear and bless
your beasts and singing birds:
And guard with tenderness
Small things that have no words.
—Traditional children's prayer of blessing

Massey Hamilton Shepherd Jr.

God of love and mercy, help us to understand our children as they grow in years and in knowledge of your world. Make us compassionate toward their temptations and failures and encouraging in their seeking after truth and value for their lives. Stir in us appreciation of their ideals and sympathy in their frustrations; that with them we may look for a better world than either we or they have known, through Jesus Christ, our common Lord and Master.

Prayer for Children

Good Shepherd who carries the lambs in your arms, we humbly ask you to give your spirit to all those engaged in training the young. Make them patient and grant them tenderness, sincerity, and firmness, and enable them to lead the young hearts to you, for your name's sake.

Short Memos to God

Heavenly Father, bless our children with healthful bodies, with good understandings, with the grace and gifts of your Spirit, with sweet dispositions and holy habits.

—Jeremy Taylor

Mary Batchelor

Lord, we give into your care our children who are causing us so much worry. The days are gone when we could correct them and tell them what to do. Now that they are grown up we have to stand by and watch them making mistakes and doing what is foolish or wrong.

Thank you that you have gone on loving and forgiving us, your wayward children, over many years. Help us to be loving and forgiving to our own children. Help us never to stop praying for them. We earnestly ask you to bring them back to yourself and us.

Ease our own torment and distress, and give us peace in trusting you, especially in the dark hours of the night. You are our heavenly Father, who loves our children more than we do and we bring them to you now, in Jesus' name.

Short Memos to God

Father, help us as parents to look to you, the one perfect Father, as an example of how to bring up our children knowing and loving you for who you are.

—Source unknown

Mother's Prayer (Source Unknown)

Dear Lord, it's such a hectic day,
With little time to stop and pray,
For life's been anything but calm
Since You called me to be a Mom.

Running errands, matching socks,
Building dreams with wooden blocks,
Cooking, cleaning, finding shoes
And other stuff that children lose.

Fitting lids on bottled bugs,
Wiping tears and giving hugs,
A stack of last week's mail to read
So where's the quiet time I need?

Yet, when I steal a moment, Lord,
Just at the sink or ironing board,
To ask the blessings of Your grace,
I see them, in my small one's face.

That you have blessed me all the while
And I stoop to kiss that precious smile.

Parents' Prayer (Source Unknown)

O Lord, omnipotent Father, we give you thanks for having given us children. They are our joy, and we accept with serenity the worries, fears, and labors that bring us pain. Help us to love them sincerely. Through us you gave life to them; from eternity you knew them and loved them. Give us the wisdom to guide them, patience to teach them, vigilance to accustom them to the good through our example.

Support our love so that we may receive them back when they have strayed and make them good. It is often so difficult to understand them, to be as they would want us to be, to help them go on their way. Grant that they may always see our home as a haven in their time of need. Teach us and help us, O good Father, through the merits of Jesus, your Son and our Lord.

Short Memos to God

Thank you for the world so sweet.
Thank you for the things we eat.
Thank you for the birds that sing.
Thank you, God, for everything.

—Traditional children's prayer of thanks

Priest's Prayer Book

Lord Jesus Christ, who took little children in your arms and blessed them: bless, we ask you, all little children dear to us. Take them into the arms of your everlasting mercy, keep them from all evil, and bring them into the company of those who ever behold the face of your Father in heaven—to the glory of your holy name.

Sources

A

Addison, Joseph (1672–1719)   British author and politician.

Aderley, James (1861–1942)   British clergyman and activist.

Aitken, William H. M. H. (1841–1927)   Evangelist and missionary.

Alcuin of York (735–804)   British scholar, educator, and churchman.

Alford, Henry (1810–1871)   English churchman, writer, and theologian.

Alfred the Great (849–899)   King of Wessex from 871–99.

Alves, Rubem (b. 1933)   Brazilian theologian, writer, philosopher.

Ambrose of Milan (340–397)   An influential and powerful ruler of the fourth-century church in his home of Milan, Italy.

Anderson, Vienna Cobb (b. ?)   Author of *Prayers of our Hearts in Words and Action* (Crossroad Publishing Co., 1991).

Andrewes, Lancelot (1555–1628)   Anglican clergyman and scholar.

Queen Anne of Britain and Ireland (1665–1714)   First sovereign of Great Britain.

Anselm of Canterbury (1033–1109)   Widely influential medieval theologian and philosopher who was Archbishop of Canterbury from 1093–1109.

Aquinas, Thomas (1225–1274)   Italian Roman Catholic philosopher and theologian. Author of the *Summa Theologica*.

Arndt, Johann (1555–1621)   German Lutheran theologian.

Arnold, Gottfried (1666–1714)   German Protestant theologian.

Arnold, Thomas (1795–1842)   Influential British educator and writer.

Asa   The third king of Judah following the division of Israel into two kingdoms.

Astley, Sir Jacob (1579–1652)   Royalist commander in the English Civil War.

Augustine of Hippo (354–430)   Bishop from North Africa who was among the most important Christian leaders of the early church. Author of *The City of God*.

B

Bacon, Francis (1561–1626)   English philosopher, scientist, and statesman.

Baillie, John (1886–1960)   Scottish theologian who taught in the United States.

Barclay, William (1907–1978)   Scottish-born theologian, writer, and broadcaster.

Saint Barnabas (d. 61)   Apostolic-era evangelist from Cyprus who is believed to have become a Christian shortly after Pentecost (around 30 C.E.).

Basil of Caesarea, or Basil the Great (330–379)   Fourth-century Bishop of Caesarea.

Batchelor, Mary (b. ?)   Modern-day Christian author of *The Lion Prayer Collection* (Lion Publishing, 1992).

Baxter, Richard (1615–1691) Well-known British clergyman.

Becon, Thomas (c. 1513–1567) Chaplain of Archbishop Thomas Cranmer and writer/poet.

Beecher, Henry Ward (1813–1887) Dramatist and Protestant preacher who attempted to reconcile evolution and Christianity.

Beethoven, Ludwig van (1770–1827) German composer.

Benedict of Nursia (c. 480–c. 540) Italian-born theologian who founded western monasticism.

Benson, Edward White (1829–1896) Academic and Archbishop of Canterbury.

Bernard of Clairvaux (1090–1153) Twelfth-century French monk.

Bersier, Eugène (1830–1903) French Reformed minister in Paris.

Bonar, Andrew (1810–1892) Nineteenth-century Scottish preacher and writer.

Bonar, Horatius (1808–1889) Nineteenth-century minister in the Church of Scotland. Brother of Andrew Bonar.

Bonaventure (1221–1274) The leader of the Franciscans after the death of their founder, Francis of Assisi.

Bonhoeffer, Dietrich (1906–1945) German theologian whose opposition to Nazism led to his execution.

Borgia, Francis (1510–1572) Friend and advisor of Ignatius of Loyola. Served as a Jesuit missionary.

The Book of Cerne Ninth-century Anglo-Saxon prayer book.

Book of Common Prayer There are several prayer books by this title, compiled for different time periods, denominations, and cultures. Originally written by Thomas Cranmer (1489–1556), who helped found the Anglican Church.

Book of Common Worship A companion to the *Book of Common Prayer*, it contains commonly used worship liturgies.

A Book of Hours The main prayer book used throughout the day in medieval Europe.

Bradstreet, Anne (1612–1672) Early American poet.

Bradwardine, Thomas (1290–1349) An archbishop from England, sometimes called "the Profound Doctor."

Brainerd, David (1718–1747) Presbyterian missionary to Native Americans.

Bright, William (1824–1901) Well-known church historian and writer.

Bromfield, Louis (1896–1956) Prize-winning American author and scientific farmer.

Brontë, Anne (1820–1849) British author/poet.

Brooks, Philips (1835–1893) Noted Episcopalian minister in Philadelphia.

Browning, Elizabeth Barrett (1806–1861) Famous poet of Victorian England.

Bunyan, John (1628–1888) English preacher and writer best known for his *Pilgrim's Progress.*

Burns, Robert (1759–1796) Scottish poet and pioneer of the Romantic Movement.

C

Calvin, John (1509–1564) Highly influential Protestant Reformation-era French Christian theologian.

Carmichael, Alexander (1832–1912) Compiler of *Carmina Gadelica,* a collection of Gaelic folk tales, songs, hymns, and prayers.

Carpenter, William Boyd (1841–1918) English clergyman and writer.

Cassian, John (360–435) Ordained a deacon of the church in Constantinople and became a monk in Bethlehem.

Catherine of Genoa (1447–1510) Italian Christian who was born to nobility but who devoted her life to ministering to the sick.

Catherine of Siena (1347–1386) Fourteenth-century mystic who devoted her life to serving the sick.

Celebrating Common Prayer   A series of prayer books by the Society of St. Francis.

Celts   A number of ancient European ethnic groups, mainly located in the British Isles, who used the Celtic languages.

Challoner, Richard (1691–1781)   English-born Roman Catholic writer and clergyman.

Chambers, Oswald (1874–1917)   Scottish-born teacher/preacher and also prolific writer.

Chao, T. C. (1888–1979)   Chinese Christian theologian.

King Charles I (1600–1649)   King of England, Scotland, and Ireland from 1625 until his execution in 1649.

Chesterton, Gilbert Keith (1874–1936)   Prolific British Christian writer of both fiction and nonfiction.

Christian Aid   An organization that works in more than fifty countries helping people of all races and religions.

Chrysostom, John (c. 345–407)   Known as "the Golden Mouth" because of his eloquent and powerful preaching, he was a contemporary of Ambrose.

Clare of Assisi (1194–1253)   Co-founder of the Order of Poor Ladies, or the Poor Clares.

Coleridge, Mary Elizabeth (1861–1907)   British poet.

Coleridge, Samuel Taylor (1772–1834)   English poet and philosopher.

Colet, John (1467?–1519)   English scholar, teacher, and priest who influenced the approach to learning and Bible study in the church.

Collyer, Robert (1823–1912)   American minister who worked in both Chicago and New York.

Saint Columba (c. 521–597)   Irish missionary monk who helped reintroduce Christianity to Scotland.

Columbanus (543–615)   Irish missionary who founded a number of monasteries throughout Europe.

de la Colombière, Claude (1641–1682)   French Missionary and ascetic writer.

Cooper, Anthony Ashley (1801–1885)   Influential British philanthropist and seventh Earl of Shaftesbury.

Cosin, John (1594–1672)   Anglican bishop of Durham as well as theologian and liturgist.

Coverdale, Miles (1488–1568)   Bishop of Exeter, England, who is famous for translating the Bible into English in 1535.

Cowman, Mrs. Charles (1870–1960)   Served with her husband as missionary to China and Japan.

Cowper, William (1731–1800)   English poet and hymn writer.

Cranmer, Thomas (1489–1556)   First Protestant Bishop of Canterbury, making him the leader of the Church of England.

Cromwell, Oliver (1599–1658)   Led the armed forces of Parliament to victory in the English Civil War (1640s) and ruled England from 1653–1658.

D

King David   Israel's second and most famous and influential king.

Dawson, George (1821–1876)   English nonconformist preacher.

Doddridge, Philip (1702–1751)   English nonconformist preacher and hymn writer.

Donne, John (1572–1631)   Great English poet, preacher, and Dean of St. Paul's Cathedral.

E

Eastern Orthodox Church   A body of Christianity that includes Greek and Russian Orthodox churches as well as others.

Edelman, Marian Wright (b. 1939)   President and founder of the Children's Defense Fund.

Edmund of Abingdon (1175–1240)   *See* Edmund Rich.

Egbert of York (d. 766)   Archbishop of York.

Queen Elizabeth I (1533–1603)   Queen of England who reigned from 1558 until her death.

Elizabeth of Hungary (1207–1231)   Princess of Hungary.

Madame Elizabeth of France (1764–1794)   Also known as Princess Elisabeth.

Emerson, Ralph Waldo (1803–1882)   One of the leading figures in American literature and involved in the Transcendentalist movement.

Ephraem of Syria (c. 306–373)   Deacon, hymn writer, and theologian of fourth-century Syria.

Erasmus of Rotterdam (1466–1536)   Dutch Renaissance scholar and forerunner of the Protestant Reformation.

Erigena, John Scotus (c. 810–c. 877)   Philosopher and theologian born in what is now Ireland.

F

Faber, Frederick William (1814–1863)   Nineteenth-century Anglican-minister turned Roman Catholic priest.

Fénelon, François (1651–1715)   French Roman Catholic theologian, writer, and poet.

de Foucauld, Charles (1856–1916)   A Trappist monk who later served the Poor Clares in Nazareth and Jerusalem. Later he became a priest, then a hermit.

Fox, George (1624–1691)   Englishman who founded the Society of Friends (Quakers).

Francis of Assisi (1181–1226)   Famous and influential Italian-born founder of the Franciscan order.

Fraser, Alexander Campbell (1819–1914)   Scottish philosopher.

G

Temple Gairdner of Cairo (1873–1928)   Christian missionary to Muslim people in Egypt.

Gelasian Sacramentary   A book of liturgical prayers compiled near Paris in the fifth and eighth centuries.

Gilbert of Hoyland (d. 1170)   Twelfth-century abbot of the Cistercian monastery of Swineshead, Lincolnshire, England.

Gregory the Great (540–604)   First monk to be promoted to the position of pope, in 590.

Gregory of Nazianzus (329–389)   Fourth-century bishop of Constantinople. Also known as Gregory the Theologian.

Gregory of Nyssa (c. 330–395)   A Christian bishop in Nyssa (in modern-day Turkey).

Gregorian Sacramentary   A fifth-century liturgical book accredited to Gregory the Great. There are many versions of it available.

Grindal, Edmund (c. 1519–1583)   English church leader who held the positions of Bishop of London, Archbishop of York, and Archbishop of Canterbury.

Guigo the Carthusian (d. 1188)   A member of the Carthusian order and a proponent and teacher of prayer.

H

Haldane, Robert (1764–1842   Scottish churchman and writer.

Hammarskjöld, Dag (1905–1961)   Swedish-born Secretary General of the United Nations from 1953—1961.

Hammond, Henry (1605–1660)   English churchman, scholar, and preacher.

Hauerwas, Stanley (b. 1940)   Modern-day United Methodist theologian and ethicist. Author of *Prayers Plainly Spoken* (Intervarsity Press, 1999).

Havergal, Frances Ridley (1836–1879)   English Christian poet and hymn writer.

Henry, Matthew (1662–1714)   English nonconformist (non-Anglican) clergyman who wrote the popular Bible commentary that bears his name.

King Henry VI (1421–1471)   King of England from 1422–1461.

Herbert, George (1593–1633)   Anglican clergyman and one of the leading English Metaphysical poets of his time.

Hippolytus of Rome (c. 190–236)   A priest in the church in Rome in the late second and early third centuries.

Hopkins, Gerard Manley (1844–1889)   Nineteenth-century English poet and Roman Catholic monk.

Hornby, Wilfred (years unknown)   Sixth bishop of the church in Nassau, the Bahamas, from 1904–18.

Hughes, Gerard W. (b. 1924)   Writer and teacher who is an ordained Jesuit priest.

O'Huiginn, Tadhg (d. 1448)   Irish poet.

Hunter, John (1849–1917)   Minister and teacher in the nineteenth and twentieth centuries.

I

Ignatius of Antioch (c. 30–107)   The third bishop or Patriarch of Antioch. Died a martyr.

Ignatius of Loyola (1491–1556)   Spanish-born-and-raised founder of the Jesuits.

Irenaeus of Lyons (c. 130–200)   Bishop of Lugdunum in Gaul, which is now Lyons, France.

Isaac the Great of Syria (d. 460)   Prolific writer of theological literature and history and likely the priest of an independent Syrian church.

Isidore of Seville (560–636)   Archbishop of Seville (southern Spain) for more than three decades.

J

Jenks, Benjamin (1646–1724)   British theological writer and clergyman.

Saint Jerome (c. 342–420)   Church father who translated the Bible from its original languages of Hebrew and Greek into Latin.

Jewel, John (1522–1571)   British clergyman who was appointed Bishop of Salisbury in 1560.

John of the Cross (1542–1591)   A Spanish mystic and Carmelite friar and a major figure in the Roman Catholic Reformation.

John of Kronstadt (1829–1908)   Archpriest of the Russian Orthodox Church.

John of Ruysbroeck (1293–1381)   A Flemish mystic Christian, known as "Admirable Doctor."

Pope John Paul II (1920–2005)   Catholic pope from 1978 until his death.

Jowett, John Henry (1864–1923)   English Congregationalist and writer/educator.

Julian of Norwich (c. 1342–1420)   Christian mystic who is famous for her book *Sixteen Revelations of Divine Love*.

K

Kempe, Margery (1373–1438)   Author of *The Book of Margery*, which is considered by some to be the first autobiography in the English language.

à Kempis, Thomas (1380–1471)   A Christian monk best known for his book *Imitation of Christ*.

Ken, Thomas (1637–1711)   English bishop and hymn writer.

Kierkegaard, Søren (1813–1855)   Danish theologian and existentialist philosopher.

Kingsley, Charles (1819–1875)   English novelist/clergymen/activist.

Knox, John (c. 1513–1572)   Fiery preacher who led the Protestant Reformation in Scotland.

L

Laud, William (1573–1645)   A key figure in the Church of England leading up to the outbreak of the English Civil War.

Leighton, Robert (1611–1684)   A Presbyterian preacher in Scotland.

Leo the Great (d. 461)   Became pope in 440.

Leofric (1016–1072)   Bishop of Exeter, England.

Leonine Sacramentary   The oldest known sacramentary, or liturgical book, dating back to the seventh century.

Libertines   A party of opposition to John Calvin's rule and reform in the city of Geneva.

Lincoln, Abraham (1809–1865)   Sixteenth president of the United States (1861–1865).

Livingstone, David (1813–1873)   Victorian-era Scottish missionary and explorer.

Ludolf of Saxony (c. 1300–c. 1378)   Author of *Life of Christ* and is believed to have influenced Thomas à Kempis.

Luther, Martin (1483–1546)   A Catholic monk whose 95 Theses sparked the Protestant Reformation.

M

Malabar Liturgy   Catholic liturgy used in India. Dated to sixteenth century.

Marshall, Catherine (1914–1983)   Wife of Presbyterian minister Peter Marshall and noted Christian author and speaker.

Marshall, Peter (1902–1949)   Presbyterian minister who emigrated to the U.S. from Scotland. Served as chaplain to the United States Senate.

Martineau, James (1805–1900)   British born Unitarian minister.

Martyn, Henry (1781–1812)   English missionary to India.

Maurice, Frederick D. (1805–1872)   English theologian and scholar.

Mayer, Rupert (1876–1945)   German Jesuit priest and leader in Roman Catholic resistance to the Third Reich.

McCheane, Arthur Henry (b. 1921)   British chaplain and pastor.

Mechthild of Magdeburg (1210–1280)   Medieval mystic and Cistercian nun whose book described her visions of God.

Meditations on the Cross   One of several books by this title.

Melanchthon, Philipp (1467–1560)   German scholar and humanist who was the chief associate of Martin Luther.

Melania the Younger (383–439)   Roman born Christian who founded a monastery in Jerusalem.

Merton, Thomas (1915–1968)   Roman Catholic monk and popular spiritual writer.

Michelangelo (1475–1564)   One of the most famous artists in history. Worked in marble mainly, but was also a great painter, architect, and poet.

Miller, J. R. (1840–1912)   Prolific American author/writer/publisher.

Millman, Robert (1816–1876)   Nineteenth-century Bishop of Calcutta, India.

Milner–White, Eric (1884–1963)   Dean of King's College, Cambridge, and York.

Milton, John (1608–1674)   English poet and political writer. Author of *Paradise Lost*.

Moody, D. L. (1837–1899)   One of the greatest American preachers/evangelists of all time.

Moore, Thomas (1779–1852)   Irish poet who wrote lyrics for some the most-beloved songs in the English language.

More, Sir Thomas (1478–1535)   English statesman, scholar, and lawyer in the reign of Henry VIII.

Morgan, George Campbell (1863–1945)   English preacher and Bible teacher.

Moule, H. C. G. (1841–1920)   English educator and spiritual leader.

Mozarabic Liturgy   A form of worship within the Latin Rite of the church, dating to the seventh and eighth centuries.

Münzer, Thomas (1490–1525)   Reformation-era Roman Catholic priest who later turned to Protestantism.

Murray, Andrew (1828–1917)   Scottish missionary to South Africa.

N

Neale, John Mason (1818–1866)   English hymn writer and religious historian.

Newman, John Henry (1801–1890)   A Church of England scholar and preacher who converted to Roman Catholicism in 1845 and became a cardinal in 1879.

Newton, John (1725–1807)   English slave trader who repented and became an Anglican clergyman and writer. Wrote the hymn "Amazing Grace."

Nicholas of Flüe (1417–1487)   Swiss hermit who is the patron saint of Switzerland.

Niebuhr, Reinhold (1892–1971)   Prominent American theologian/philosopher.

Nightingale, Florence (1820–1910)   Italian-born nurse who used her skills to minister to those in poverty.

Nitobe, Inazo (1862–1933)   Japanese Christian, agriculturist, philosopher, educator, and political activist.

O

Orchard, William Edwin (1877–1955)   Roman Catholic priest and theologian.

Orthodox Church   Church bodies or churches, most of which are associated with Eastern churches, including the Eastern Orthodox Church and the Russian Orthodox Church.

Orthodox Prayer Book   One of several prayer books for the Orthodox churches.

Owen, David M. (years unknown)   Minister in the United Reformed Church.

Oxenden, Ashton (1808–1892)   Nineteenth-century clergyman with the Church of England.

Oxenham, John (1852–1941)   Pen name of William Arthur Dunkerley, a British journalist, novelist, and poet.

P

Pascal, Blaise (1623–1662)   French mathematician, physicist, philosopher, and theologian.

Parsons, Edward Lambe (1868–1960)   Episcopal Bishop of California.

Paton, Alan Stewart (1903–1988)   South African author and activist who founded the South African Liberal Party, which fought against apartheid.

Saint Patrick (386–493)   Christian missionary considered Ireland's patron saint.

Patrick, Simon (1626–1707)   British divine who was appointed dean of Peterborough in 1679 and Bishop of Chichester in England in 1689.

The Apostle Paul   The biblical apostle to the Gentiles and writer of much of the New Testament texts.

Philaret of Moscow (1782–1867)   Archpastor of the Russian Orthodox Church.

Pilkington, James (c. 1520–1576)   Anglican Bishop of Durham from 1561 until his death in 1576.

Polycarp (69–155)   Bishop of the church in Smyrna—a city today known as Izmir. He died a martyr.

The Prayer Book   A long line of liturgical books for several Christian denominations.

Priest's Prayer Book   Prayer book used by priests.

Pusey, Edward Bouverie (1800–1882)   English theologian and one of the leaders of the Oxford Movement.

R

Rauschenbusch, Walter (1861–1918)   American Baptist minister and theology professor.

Rich, Edmund (1180–1240)   Archbishop of Canterbury in 1234.

Richard of Chichester (1197–1253)   Thirteenth-century Bishop of Chichester.

Rolle, Richard (c. 1290–1349)   English mystical hermit and poet.

The Roman Breviary   Official liturgy of public worship for the Roman Catholic Church.

The Roman Catholic *Family Prayer Book*   A regularly updated collection of prayers for Roman Catholic families.

Rossetti, Christina (1830–1894)   Anglican poet.

Routh, Martin J. (1755–1834)   President of Magdalen College in Oxford.

S

Sandburg, Carl (1878–1967)   American poet, biographer.

Sarum Primer   Collection of prayers and worship resources developed in the thirteenth century in Salisbury, England.

Schweitzer, Albert (1875–1965)   Medical missionary and theologian.

Scudamore, William Edward (1813–1881)   Author and rector of Ditchingham.

Scriven, Joseph (1819–1886)   Irish-born Christian hymn writer.

Seraphim of Sarov (1759–1833)   Russian Orthodox priest and hermit.

Serapion of Thmuis (d. after 360)   Bishop of Thmuis in the Nile Delta.

Seton, Elizabeth Ann (1774–1821)   American educator who formed several charities.

Shakespeare, William (1564–1616)   English playwright.

Shepherd, Massey Hamilton, Jr. (1913–1990)   American liturgist and educator.

Simons, Menno (1492–1559)   Dutch Anabaptist whose teachings helped form the Mennonites.

Singh, Sadhu Sundar (1889–1929?)   Indian Christian convert and missionary to Tibet.

Smart, Christopher (1722–1771)   Eighteenth-century English poet.

Smith, Hannah Whitall (1832–1911)   Lay speaker and author related to the Holiness movement in the United States and Higher Life movement in England.

Spafford, Horatio Gates (1828–1888)   American lawyer who spent much of his own money helping victims of the Chicago fire.

Spurgeon, Charles Haddon (1834–1892)   One of the greatest Christian preachers/evangelists of his time.

Stevenson, Robert Louis (1850–1894)   Famous Scottish novelist/poet.

Suso, Henry (1296–1366)   German mystic and Dominican.

Swindoll, Charles (b. 1934)   American pastor, author, educator, and radio preacher.

Symeon the New Theologian (949–1022)   Abbot of St. Mamas in Constantinople. Born in Asia Minor (now Turkey).

T

Tabb, John Banister (1845–1909)   American poet and priest.

Tagore, Rabindranath (1861–1941)   Influential cultural figure in modern India. Won 1913 Nobel Prize in literature.

Tauler, Johannes (c. 1300–1361)   German mystic, theologian, and writer.

Taylor, James Hudson (1832–1905)   English-born missionary to China.

Taylor, Jeremy (1613–1667)   Native Briton who at one point served the chaplain to King Charles I and to the Royalist army.

Temple, William (1881–1944)   Archbishop of York and later Canterbury.

ten Boom, Corrie (1892–1983)   Dutch Christian Holocaust survivor who helped many Jews escape the Nazis during World War II.

Tennyson, Alfred Lord (1809–1892)   Famous British-born poet.

Teresa of Avila (1515–1582)   Member and reformer of the Carmelite order. One of the foremost Christian mystics.

Mother Teresa of Calcutta (1910–1997)   One of the best-known twentieth-century Christian servants to the poor.

Tersteegen, Gerhard (1697–1769)   German Christian writer.

Tileston, Mary Wilder (1843–1934)   Devotional compiler of spiritual literature.

Toplady, Augustus Montague (1740–1778)   Anglican hymn writer and poet, best known for "Rock of Ages."

Tozer, A. W. (1897–1963)   American pastor and author.

Traherne, Thomas (1636–1674)   English poet and Christian writer.

Treasury of Devotion   An early twentieth century collection of devotions and prayers.

Tychon of Zadonsk (1724–1783)   Russian Orthodox bishop and vicar.

V

Van Buren, Abigail (b. 1918)   Columnist of column titled "Dear Abby."

Vaughan, Henry (1622–1695)   English poet.

The Venerable Bede (673–735)   Benedictine monk, author, and scholar at the Northumbrian monastery in England.

Vianney, Jean-Baptiste Marie (1786–1859)   French priest and patron saint of parish priests.

The Victorines   Twelfth-century writers who produced a systematic teaching on meditation.

Bora, Katherine von (1499–1552)   German Catholic nun who embraced Lutheran theology and married Martin Luther in 1525.

W

Washington, George (1732–1799)   First president of the United States.

Watts, Isaac (1674–1748)   English clergyman and prolific hymn writer.

Wesley, Charles (1707–1788)   Leader of the Methodist movement, but best known as a prolific writer of Christian hymns.

Wesley, John (1703–1791)   Older brother of Charles and also one of the greatest traveling evangelists in the history of Christianity.

Wesley, Samuel (1662–1735)   English poet and hymn writer and father of John and Charles Wesley.

Westcott, Brooke Foss (1825–1901)   English churchman and theologian who served as bishop of Durham from 1890 until his death.

Westminster Confession of Faith (1647)   Reformed confession of faith drawn up by the Westminster Assembly.

Whittier, John Greenleaf (1807–1892)   American Quaker poet and abolitionist.

Wilson, Antoinette   Poet quoted in early twentieth-century devotional *Streams in the Desert* by Mrs. Charles Cowman.

Wilson, Thomas (1663–1755)   Bishop of Sodor and Man.

Woolman, John (1720–1772)   A member of the Society of Friends (Quakers) and active abolitionist.

World Vision   International Christian relief and aid organization.

X

Xavier, Francis (1506–1552)   Spanish missionary to China and the co-founder, with Ignatius, of the Jesuit order.

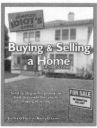

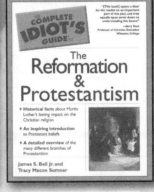